More Sower's Seeds

Second Planting

by

Brian Cavanaugh, T.O.R.

Paulist Press
New York   Mahwah

Library of Congress Cataloging-in-Publication Data

More Sower's seeds: second planting/[edited] by Brian Cavanaugh.—
  [Rev. ed.]
    p. cm.
  Rev. ed. of: The Sower's seeds. c1990.
  Includes index.
  ISBN 0-8091-3324-5 (pbk.)
  1. Homiletical illustrations. I. Cavanaugh, Brian, 1947– . II. Sower's seeds.
  BV4225.2.S6 1992
  251'.08—dc20
                                  92-12675
                                  CIP

Published by Paulist Press
997 Macarthur Boulevard
Mahwah, NJ 07430

Printed and bound in the
United States of America

Contents

Dedication

This book is dedicated to the students of Saint Francis College, especially those in the Honors Program, who have dutifully put up with my storytelling attempts through preaching, teaching and public speaking. Thank you for keeping me sharp.

Acknowledgments

I am grateful for all those people who purchased a copy of my first book *The Sower's Seeds*. I appreciate the letters of encouragement and requests for more stories.

I am grateful for the people-in-the-pew who listen to these stories, and for relating how they have meaning for them.

I especially thank Donna Menis, once again, for her invaluable editing of the manuscript and insightful suggestions.

Introduction

"Collecting Stories"

Frequently I'm asked, "Where do you find all your stories?" My response is simple, "How is it that you miss them?" Stories abound! They are around you everywhere, almost like the wind. Well, at least for those who have "eyes to see and ears to hear." Jesus, a master storyteller, would see a farmer on the hill, or a field ripe for the harvest, or recall the preparations for a marriage banquet and he would use them to illustrate whatever point he was trying to make. He didn't have access to a reference library or a collection of story books. Jesus did have, however, a keen sense of observation and awareness. He not only saw or heard something, but he was also able to incorporate it meaningfully. As Zorba the Greek says, "If only I could never open my mouth until the abstract idea had reached its highest point—and became a story."

A recent DISCOVERY television program revealed that when parent penguins return to the rookery, where there are hundreds, or even thousands, of seemingly identical adult penguins and chicks, the parent quickly finds its own chick by hearing the singular sound of its voice. Amidst the cacophony of all the clattering chirps, parents and chicks are able to find each other by focusing in on this unique sound. Discovering stories employs a similar technique. When reading—reading anything—watching television, listening to or observing others, attention needs to be focused on discovering any information which might be turned into a story. A person's individual awareness needs to be expanded and one's imagination sensitized. Discovering stories for me is as if a little bell rings inside my head saying—*pay attention*.

The next step in collecting stories is to notate the story by a pencil mark in the margin, or by jotting down a few key phrases, or by making notes into a recorder, or whatever other means one can employ to capture the gist of the story. This process tends to become second nature as a person learns to focus one's attention on finding stories.

The last step is the hardest part in collecting stories. It is writing the story into a notebook. Most people can easily find a story. A good many people somehow make a mental note of a story. Yet very few take the time necessary to write the story into a composition book. Complete discipline and time are required to capture a story, to refine it, to re-work it, and to turn it into a meaningful illustration.

There isn't a magic formula to finding and collecting stories. Story collecting, in many ways, follows the laws of creation. God created humans with two eyes, two ears and only one mouth. If an individual used them more in direct proportion, rather than inversely, he or she would develop the "eyes to see and ears to hear."

1.
The Eagle and the Rattlesnake

Anonymous

There is a great battle that rages inside every person.

One side is the soaring eagle. Everything the eagle stands for is good and true and beautiful. The eagle soars high above the clouds. Even though it dips down into the valleys, the eagle builds its nest on the mountaintops.

The other side is the slithering serpent, the rattlesnake. That crafty, deceitful snake represents the worst aspects of a person—the darker side. The snake feeds upon one's downfalls and setbacks, and justifies itself by its presence in the slithering mass.

Who wins this great battle in your life? None other than the one that is fed the most—the eagle, or the rattlesnake.

2.
The Plimsoll Line

Anonymous

Samuel Plimsoll was a member of the British Parliament about a century ago. He was distressed because cargo ships were being loaded so heavily that they sank at sea, with much loss of life and property. So he got a law passed requiring danger lines to be painted on all cargo ships. When the weight of the cargo lowered the ship down to where the line touched the water, all loading had to stop. Seamen still call this mark the "Plimsoll line."

People also have Plimsoll lines—a point where for the

sake of health, happiness and plain common sense, we should not attempt to shoulder more responsibility, however important, than we can intelligently handle.

3.
Listening . . . Paying Attention!

Hank Ketcham

Several years ago I read a "Dennis The Menace" comic strip that caught my attention. In the first panel, Dennis with his dog, Ruff, at his side, is walking along with Margaret. Dennis is merrily pulling a red wagon, while Margaret, clutching her doll, is jabbering to the wind.

In the second panel, Dennis gives Ruff a slinky, side-long glance while Margaret's prattle continues. However, she is now speaking directly in Dennis' ear.

The third scene shows Margaret wildly pelting Dennis with her doll saying, "Dennis, you're not listening to me when I'm speaking to you."

The final panel has Dennis turning towards Margaret saying, "Margaret, I'm listening to you, it's just that I'm not paying any attention!"

4.
Good Luck . . . Bad Luck?

Anonymous

Many years ago there was an old man who had one son and a horse. One day his horse broke out of the corral and fled to the freedom of the hills. "Your horse got out? What bad luck!" said his neighbors.

"Why do you say that?" asked the old man. "How do you know it's bad luck?"

Sure enough, the next night the horse came back to his

4

familiar corral for his usual feeding and watering, leading twelve wild horses with him. The farmer's son saw the horses in the corral, slipped out a side door and locked the gate. Suddenly the farmer and his son had thirteen horses instead of none. The neighbors heard the good news and rushed to the farmer, "Thirteen horses! What good luck you have."

The old farmer answered, "How do you know that it's good luck?"

Some days later his strong young son was trying to ride one of the wild horses, only to be thrown off and break a leg. The neighbors came back that night and passed another hasty judgment: "Your son broke his leg. What bad luck."

The wise father answered again, "How do you know it's bad luck?"

Sure enough, a few days later a warlord came through the town and conscripted every able-bodied young man, taking them off to war, never to return to their homes again. But the young man was saved because of his broken leg.

5.
'Twas the Night Before Jesus Came

Anonymous

'Twas the night before Jesus came and all through the house
    not a creature was praying, not one in the house.

Their Bibles were lain on the shelf without care,
    in hopes that Jesus would not come there.

The children were dressing to crawl into bed,
    not once ever kneeling or bowing a head;

And mom in her rocker with baby on her lap,
    was watching the late show while I took a nap;

When out of the East there arose such a clatter,
    I sprang to my feet to see what was the matter;

5

Away to the window I flew like a flash,
  threw open the shutters and threw up the sash.
The light of His face made me cover my head,
  it was Jesus returning, just like He said.
And though I possessed worldly wisdom and wealth,
  I cried when I saw Him in spite of myself.
In the book of life, which He held in His hand,
  was written the name of every saved man.
He spoke not a word as He searched for my name,
  when He said, "It's not here!" my head hung in
    shame.
The people whose names had been written with love,
  He gathered to take to His Father above.
With those who were ready He rose without a sound,
  while all the rest were left standing around.
I fell to my knees, but it was too late:
  I had waited too long and thus sealed my fate.
I stood and I cried as they rose out of sight.
  Oh, if only I had been ready tonight.
In the words of this poem the meaning is clear,
  the coming of Jesus is drawing near.
There's only one life and when the last name is called,
  we'll find that the Bible was true after all.

6.
The Beggar King
Anonymous

Once there was a time, according to legend, when Ireland was ruled by a king who had no son. The king sent out his couriers to post notices in all the towns of his realm. The notices advised that every qualified young man should apply for an interview with the king as a possible successor to the throne. However, all such candidates must have these two qualifications: They must (1) love God and (2) love their fellow human beings.

The young man about whom this legend centers saw a notice and reflected that he loved God and, also, his neighbors. One thing stopped him, he was so poor that he had no clothes that would be presentable in the sight of the king. Nor did he have the funds to buy provisions for the long journey to the castle. So the young man begged here, and borrowed there, finally managing to scrounge enough money for the appropriate clothes and the necessary supplies.

Properly attired and well-suited, the young man set out on his quest, and had almost completed the journey when he came upon a poor beggar by the side of the road. The beggar sat trembling, clad only in tattered rags. His extended arms pleaded for help. His weak voice croaked, "I'm hungry and cold. Please help me . . . please?"

The young man was so moved by this beggar's need that he immediately stripped off his new clothes and put on the tattered threads of the beggar. Without a second thought he gave the beggar all his provisions as well. Then, somewhat hesitantly, he continued his journey to the castle dressed in the rags of the beggar, lacking provisions for his return trek home. Upon his arrival at the castle, a king's attendant showed him in to the great hall. After a brief respite to clean off the journey's grime, he was finally admitted to the throne room of the king.

The young man bowed low before his majesty. When he raised his eyes, he gaped in astonishment. "You . . . it's you! You're the beggar by the side of the road."

"Yes," the king replied with a twinkle, "I was that beggar."

"But . . . bu . . . buu . . . you are not really a beggar. You are the king for real. Well, then, why did you do this to me?" the young man stammered after gaining more of his composure.

"Because I had to find out if you genuinely love God

and your fellow human beings," said the king. "I knew that if I came to you as king, you would have been impressed by my gem-encrusted golden crown and my royal robes. You would have done anything I asked of you because of my regal character. But that way I would never have known what is truly in your heart. So I used a ruse. I came to you as a beggar with no claims on you except for the love in your heart. And I discovered that you sincerely do love God and your fellow human beings. You will be my successor," promised the king. "You will inherit my kingdom."

7.
Thomas Edison's Turnstile
Anonymous

That great inventor, Thomas A. Edison, had a keen appreciation of both time and money. Every time he showed his constant stream of visitors the new inventions and gadgets that filled his summer estate, someone was sure to ask, "Mr. Edison, why do you have that preposterous turnstile that we have to push our way through on the way to the garden?"

Edison would invariably reply happily, "My friend, every single soul who pushes his way through that turnstile pumps seven gallons of water into the holding tank on the roof."

8.
Where Are You, Lord?
Brewer Mattocks

The parish priest in a town named Austerity climbed way up in the church's steeple to be nearer to God. He wanted to hand down God's Word to his parishioners, like Moses of old. Then, one day he indeed thought he heard God say something.

The priest cried aloud from the steeple, "Where are you, Lord? I can't seem to hear your voice clearly."

And the Lord replied, "I'm down here among my people. Where are you?"

9.
African Speechmaking

Anonymous

There used to be a civilized rule about speechmaking among some African tribes. It seems that when a person rose to speak, he had to stand on one foot while delivering his oration. The moment his other foot touched the ground, the speech had to end, or the speaker was forcibly silenced.

10.
The Carpenter and the Unbuilder
(condensed)

David M. Griebner

Once upon a time there was a man living in a far-off kingdom who received an invitation from his king to come for dinner. He was excited by the invitation. However, he was afraid as well. Would his manners be good enough for his lord's table? What would they talk about when they were not eating? Above all, the man was frightened by the long journey across the kingdom to the king's castle.

So what did he do? Well, he spent one month deciding what to wear. He spent two months learning the rules of etiquette, and practicing them as he ate. He spent three months reading up on all the latest issues faced by the kingdom so he would have something to say.

Finally, he faced the journey itself. By trade the man was a carpenter. He built small houses, add-ons, and garages better than anyone else. After he had packed the clothing and food he thought he would need for the journey, he had room for only a little more. So he decided to pack a few tools, enough to permit him to build adequate overnight shelter. Then he started out.

The first day he traveled long and hard . . . stopping only to eat a bit of lunch. Then he set about constructing a rough shelter to spend the night in. After a few hours' labor he had a small, safe, dry place to sleep. The next morning, as he was about to start out again, he noticed places where the shelter could be made better. So, instead of resuming the journey right away, he began to make improvements on his little dwelling. One thing led to another, garage to kitchen, to study and indoor plumbing, and so on. Soon he had pretty much forgotten about the invitation.

Meanwhile, the king began to wonder about the man. And as kings are able to do, he arranged for another person who was also traveling to the dinner to stop by and see how the man was coming along.

When he found the man, the carpenter was living in his second house. He had sold the first one, remembered the invitation, and moved on for a day or so. However, soon he had settled in and built a bigger and better house on the profits from the sale of his first house. The carpenter was only too happy to invite the visitor in for lunch, but while he was content to accept the offer of food, the visitor preferred to eat out in the yard under a tree.

"Is there a reason why you don't want to come in?" asked the carpenter.

"Why, yes," replied the other. "You see, I'm on a journey to have dinner with the king of our land. It is important for me to stay on the journey. Perhaps, after lunch, you would like to come with me?"

"What you say sounds familiar to me," said the carpenter. "I think I too received an invitation to have dinner with the king, but I have been a little bit uncertain of the way."

"I know," said the stranger. "I was uncertain once as

well. As a matter of fact, once I was a carpenter just like you. I wanted to build safe places along the way to stay in. One day, another fellow on the journey helped me to learn how to unbuild instead of to build. He helped me to leave the home I had been living in and trust the journey itself. I was worried about following the right path. He told me that there were a number of paths that would lead to the castle. The king had set it up that way, and the king had also set up warnings along the wrong paths. The important thing was just to continue to put one foot in front of the other with love and trust."

"So what do you say? Why don't you let go of this house and get on with the journey?" the visitor asked.

"I don't know," replied the carpenter. "Maybe. Can I sleep on it? Can I fix a bed for you?"

"No," said the visitor. "I'll just stay out here under the tree. It is easier to notice the wonderful things the king has put along the way when you aren't looking out from inside of something which you have erected to protect yourself."

The next morning the carpenter decided to join the visitor on his journey. "Well," said the carpenter, "which way shall we go?"

"Which way seems right to you?" asked the unbuilder. "Let's sit for a few minutes and think hard about the king. Remember the stories you have been told about him. Remember how much he loves you. Remember how much you love him. When you have remembered as clearly as you think you can, consider the paths that lie before you and see which one seems to best satisfy your longing for, and remembering of, the king. Let your desire to be with the king become more powerful in you than your uncertainty and fear about choosing the right or wrong way."

Silently they sat. . . . Slowly it began to seem as though they were already on the journey. As that feeling grew and grew, it suddenly didn't seem like any decision needed to be made. It just happened. With a deep sense of freedom they were off.

Many days went just like that, new steps out of silent beginnings and pure desires. In the stillness of their hearts they made room for the paths and the paths seemed to come to them.

Of course the carpenter still felt the need to build a home from time to time. The unbuilder made sure he understood what he was doing and then let him do it if he really wanted to. While the carpenter labored, the unbuilder, his guide and friend, would continue to practice the silent waiting in the yard, under the tree, and soon they would unbuild yet another house and begin the journey again.

In the meantime the king kept the food warm. He was very good at doing that.

11.
Be a Better Person

Anonymous

A young student approached the famous French scientist and philosopher, Blaise Pascal, and declared, "If I had your brains, I would be a better person."

Pondering the depth of that statement, Pascal paused momentarily before replying, "Be a better person, and you will have my brains."

12.
God's Pattern in Our Lives

Anonymous

A poor but honest jeweler was arrested for a crime he never committed. He was placed in a secure and well-protected prison in the center of the city. One day, after he had been imprisoned for months, his wife came to the main gate. She told the guards how her husband, the poor jeweler, was a devout and prayerful man. He would be lost without his simple prayer rug. Would they not permit him to have this single possession? The guards agreed that it would be harmless and gave him the prayer rug. Five times daily he would unroll his rug and pray.

Weeks passed, and one day the jeweler said to his jailers, "I'm bored sitting here day after day with nothing to do. I am a good jeweler and, if you will let me have some pieces of metal and some simple tools, I will make you exquisite pieces of jewelry. You can sell what I make in the bazaar and add to your low salaries as civil servants. I ask for so little— just something to fill the idle hours and keep my skill in practice."

The poorly paid jailers agreed that it would be a good arrangement. Each day they brought the jeweler some bits of silver and other metals, and a few simple tools. Each night they would remove the tools and metals and take home the jewelry that he had made for them.

Days grew into weeks, weeks into months. One bright morning when they came to the jeweler's cell, they found it empty! No sign was found of the prisoner or how he had escaped from this secure and well-protected prison.

Some time later, the real criminal was arrested for the crime of which the poor jeweler had been falsely accused. One day in the city's bazaar, one of the prison guards spotted the ex-prisoner, the jeweler. Quickly explaining that the real criminal was caught, he asked the jeweler how he had escaped. The jeweler proceeded to tell an amazing story.

The jeweler's wife had gone to the chief architect who had designed the prison. She obtained from him the blueprints to the cell door locks. She then designed a pattern and weaved it into a prayer rug. Five times each day he would pray, his head touching the rug. Slowly, he began to see that there was a design within a design, within yet another design, and it was the pattern for the lock of his cell door. From the bits of leftover metal and the simple tools, he fashioned a key and escaped!

13

13.
Are You Jesus?

Brennan Manning

Several years ago a group of salesmen went to a regional sales convention in Chicago. They assured their wives that they would be home in plenty of time for Friday's supper.

One thing led to another and the meeting ran overtime so the men had to race to the airport, tickets in hand. As they barged through the terminal, one man inadvertently kicked over a table supporting a basket of apples. Without stopping they all reached the plane in time and boarded it with a sigh of relief. All but one. He paused, got in touch with his feelings, and experienced a twinge of compassion for the girl whose apple-stand had been overturned. He waved goodbye to his companions and returned to the terminal. He was glad he did. The ten-year-old girl was blind.

The salesman gathered up the apples and noticed that several of them were battered and bruised. He reached into his wallet and said to the girl, "Here, please take this ten dollars for the damage we did. I hope it didn't spoil your day."

As the salesman started to walk away the bewildered girl called out to him, "Are you Jesus?"

He stopped in mid-stride. And he wondered.

14.
Do Something So Much

Anonymous

"Many years ago," wrote Branch Rickey, "when I was managing the St. Louis Browns, I lost a game to Detroit in the last half of the eleventh inning in a very unusual manner —nothing else like it in the annals of baseball anywhere. It was the last half of the eleventh in a tie ball game. Two men were out with nobody on the bases, when a player named Ty Cobb came to bat for Detroit."

"Cobb got a base on balls and then scored the winning run without another ball being pitched. By sheer adventure and skill he forced two wild throws by St. Louis infielders. His daring at first base, his boldness and skillful turn at second, his characteristic slide ten feet before reaching third, his quick coordination following his slide—all brought about four 'breaks' in his favor. He made what amounted to a home run out of a base on balls."

"In the very same game, there was a player on my team named Walker, a man who had all the physical qualities to be a great player. During a game in Texas, the following spring, Walker hit what should have been a home run—but was thrown out at third."

"Walker's slow start to first base, as he watched his hard line drive fall in the left-center gap, cost him twenty feet. Next, he lost another thirty feet making too wide of a turn around first toward second. Then, seeing the elusive ball on its way to the Texas prairies (the left field fence was down for repair), he slowed to a trot. This easily cost him another fifty feet, and he was now one hundred feet behind schedule."

"Suddenly the ball struck some object, a board or a stone, and bounced up into the hands of the surprised center fielder. His quick pivot and strong arm brought the throw rapidly toward third. Walker, seeing that a play could now be made on him, put on a great burst of speed. He made a splendid fall-away slide to the right, right into the very hands of the third baseman. Walker actually tagged himself out."

"In discussing the play later, everyone agreed that if Walker had not made any one of the four mistakes that he made, he would have scored or at least had a triple."

"What was the difference between Cobb and Walker? They had about the same attributes—age, weight, height, and running speed. Walker had a stronger arm than Cobb and more power at the bat. Yet one player rose to unparalleled fame; the other—obscurity. Cobb wanted to do some-

15

thing so much that nothing else mattered; Walker punched the clock."

15.
To Have a Brilliant Son
Chaim Potok

Yahweh, Master of the Universe, blest me with a brilliant son. And he cursed me with all the problems of raising him. Ah, what it is to have a brilliant son! Not a smart son, Yahweh, but a brilliant son. Joshua, a boy with a mind like a jewel. Ah, what a curse it is, what an anguish it is to have a Josh whose mind is like a pearl, like a sun.

Yahweh, when my Joshua was six years old, I saw him reading a story, he swallowed it as one swallows food or water. There was no heart in my Joshua, there was only his mind. He was a mind in a body without a heart. It was a story about a poor old man and his struggle to get to Jerusalem before he died. Ah, how that man suffered! And my Joshua enjoyed the story, he enjoyed the last terrible page because when he finished it he realized for the first time what a splendid memory he possessed. He looked at me proudly and re-told the story from memory, and I cried inside my heart.

I went outside and shouted to the Master of the Universe, "Why? What have you done to me? A mind like this I need for a son? A heart I need for a son. A soul I need for a son. Compassion I want from my son. Righteousness, mercy, strength to suffer and carry pain, that I want from my son, not a mind without a soul, without a heart."

16.
Black Pebble . . . White Pebble?
Anonymous

Many years ago, when a person who owed money could be thrown into jail, a merchant in Venice had the misfortune

16

to owe a huge sum to a mean moneylender. The money-lender, who was old and ugly, fancied the merchant's beautiful young daughter. He proposed a bargain. He said he would cancel the merchant's debt if he could have the girl instead.

Both the merchant and his daughter were horrified at the suggestion. So the cunning moneylender schemed that they let Providence decide the matter. He told them that he would put a black pebble and a white pebble into an empty bag, and then the girl would have to pick out one of the pebbles. If she chose the black pebble, she would become his wife, and her father's debt would be canceled. But if she refused to pick a pebble, her father would be thrown into jail, and she would starve with no one to look after her.

Reluctantly, the merchant agreed. They were standing on a pebble-strewn path in the merchant's garden as they talked, and the moneylender stooped down to pick up the two pebbles. As he did, the girl, sharp-eyed with fright, noticed that he picked up two black pebbles and put them into the bag. The moneylender asked the girl to pick out the pebble that was to decide her fate and that of her father.

What would you have done if you had been that girl? If you had to advise her, what would you have advised her to do?

1—The girl should refuse to take a pebble?
2—The girl should show that there are two black pebbles in the bag and expose the moneylender as a cheat?
3—The girl should take a black pebble and sacrifice herself in order to save her father from prison?

The girl in the story put her hand into the bag and drew out a pebble. But, without looking at it, she fumbled it and let the pebble fall to the path where it was immediately mixed in among all the others. "Oh, how clumsy of me," she said. "Never mind, however. If you look into the bag, you'll be able to tell which pebble I dropped by the color of the one that is remaining."

Since the remaining pebble was, of course, black, it had to be assumed that she picked the white pebble. Of course, the moneylender dared not admit his own dishonesty.

17.
In the Process of Trying

Anonymous

A small college basketball team celebrated a team mass in preparation for their first venture in the NCAA "March Madness" tournament. During the homily, the team chaplain said that ten years from now the important thing about their basketball season will not be whether they won the championship or not. The important thing will be what they became in the process of trying to win the title.

Did they become better human beings?
Did they become more loving?
Did they become more loyal to one another?
Did they become more committed?
Did they grow as a team and as individuals?

After the mass, while taking off his vestments, the priest heard the coach address his players: "Sit down a minute. Father said something that is bothering me right now. I wonder what I have helped you become in the process of trying to put together a winning season.

"Have you become better human beings?
Have you become more loving?
Have you become more loyal to one another?
Have you become more committed?

Have you grown as a team and as individuals?

"If you did, then regardless of what we do in the tournament, we are a success already. If you did not, then we have failed God, we have failed your families, we have failed your school, and we have failed one another.

"I hope to God that we have not failed. I pray to God that we have not failed."

18.
Focus Your Thinking

Anonymous

On a clear, bright sunny day take a powerful magnifying glass and a stack of newspapers and go outside for an experiment. Hold the magnifying glass over a pile of crumpled pages. Even though you are magnifying the power of the sun's rays through the glass lens, you will never start a fire—if you keep moving the glass.

But if you hold the magnifying glass still, allowing it to focus the rays in a concentrated beam of sun energy, you harness the power of the sun and multiply it through the lens—starting a fire.

Focusing also works with your power of thought! Try it and ignite your wandering ideas.

19.
Ananias the Cobbler (adapted)

David Juniper

What an exciting time to live! The news of the empty tomb still rang freshly on the ears of men and women. With each passing day new miracles were occurring.

But miracles never visited Ananias, a poor little cobbler

of Damascus. "After all, I'm only a simple cobbler who can hardly read the alphabet. A shoemaker must be content to sew sandals for the glory of God," he reminded himself.

Ananias' times of prayer were also very ordinary. There were no startling revelations—only a quiet gentle Presence. However, one noontime, just as he set down his awl and threads, something very unusual happened. A whisper stirred from within his heart.

"Ananias!"

The startled cobbler tripped over his workbench. He remained still on the clay floor. He listened to the silence, but the only sound was the wild pounding of his heart. And just as its pounding began to calm, the voice came again.

"Ananias!"

This time the little shoemaker knew who had spoken. He glanced upward and, quivering, said, "Uh, here I am, Lord."

The voice sounded with deep, quiet authority: "Arise and go to Straight Street. At the house of Judas ask for a man from Tarsus named Saul. He will be praying. In a vision he has seen a man named Ananias, and you are to place your hands on him so that he may see again."

Ananias winced. Forgetting to whom he spoke, the poor cobbler scrambled to his feet. "Lord, many people have told me about this man, and about all the terrible things he has done to your people in Jerusalem. Why he has now come to Damascus to arrest anyone who even calls upon your name," said the cobbler.

A long silence followed. Ananias sheepishly looked upward, "Lord?"

Silence. The shoemaker awkwardly shuffled his feet and cleared his throat, "Ahem, . . . Lord?"

Ananias deeply sighed and bowed his head. Abruptly, the voice spoke again, "Go, because I have chosen him to be my servant, to carry my name to the Gentiles, and to the people of Israel. I myself will show him all that he must suffer for my sake."

Ananias stumbled down the muddied alleyway outside his shop. As in a dream, he wandered toward the wealthiest quarter in Damascus. Arriving at the entrance to Judas' house he knocked timidly on the door and waited until the huge portal opened a crack. A skeptical servant peered out.

Ananias rushed in, "Please sir! I must see a man by the name of Saul."

At first the servant was startled by the frantic, disheveled shoemaker, but he quickly recovered. "See here!" he said. "The servants' entrance is around the block . . . of all the nerve." He planted his palm squarely in Ananias' face and pushed the poor man out toward the street."

The struggling cobbler screamed, at least tried, "No! I must splee a man by the nab ub Saulb. . . . Pleeb, I must splee . . ." (After all, it is difficult to be articulate when someone has his hand in your face.)

Just as the servant slammed the huge door Ananias swung his leg into its path. This actually worked in the shoemaker's favor, since the volume of his screams markedly increased. They echoed throughout the neighborhood. "Ahhgggrr! My leg," he yelled.

Then there came a deep and troubled voice from within the courtyard. "Wait! I had a vision about that man," spoke another person.

Ananias nearly panicked and forgot everything. "Oh, no," he thought. "He had a vision about me! Now I'm really in trouble."

The angry servant grabbed the shoemaker's belt and jerked him into the courtyard. There under an aging olive tree, a sightless man lay on a mat. The shoemaker's fear quietly melted away.

"Saul," said Ananias, "I have been sent by the Lord Jesus whom you heard along the way. He sent me here that

you might see again and be filled with the Holy Spirit."
Ananias stretched out his hands and touched the sightless
eyes. For a quiet moment, human history rested beneath the
hands of a cobbler. When it was accomplished, a man named
Saul had become Paul.

Some time passed before Paul began his ministry. Even
more time elapsed before the world realized the tremendous
impact of that brief moment. And so, the simple shoemaker
never knew what came of that day he extended his hands
beneath an aging olive tree.

At the very end of his life, Ananias lay on his deathbed.
He looked upward toward the shadowy sky and whispered,
"I haven't done much, Lord. A few shoes sewn . . . a few
sandals stitched. . . . But what more could be expected of a
poor cobbler?"

Suddenly, once again, that same inner voice surged
from within his heart. "Don't worry, Ananias," it said,
"about how much you have accomplished—or how little.
You were there when I needed you to be there. And that, my
little shoemaker of a saint, is all that really matters."

20.
Two Monks Traveling

Anonymous

Tanzan and Ekido were once traveling together down a
muddy road. A heavy rain saturated the area. Coming
around a bend, they met a lovely girl in a silk kimono unable
to cross the mired intersection.

"Come here, girl," said Tanzan at once. Lifting her in
his arms, he carried her over the slimy ooze and set her down
on the other side.

Ekido did not speak again until that night when they
reached a lodging temple. Then he could no longer restrain
himself. "We monks don't go near females," he told Tan-

zan, "especially not young and lovely ones. It is dangerous. Why did you do that?"

"I left the girl back there," said Tanzan. "Are you still carrying her with you?"

21.
Jesus' and Judas' Faces

Anonymous

A story is told that Leonardo da Vinci painted "The Lord's Supper" when living in Milan. Before he could paint the thirteen figures, it was necessary to find men who could serve as models. Each model had to have a face that expressed da Vinci's vision of the particular man he would represent. Needless to say, this proved to be a tedious task—to find just the right face.

One Sunday as da Vinci was at the cathedral for mass, he saw a young man in the choir who looked like da Vinci's idea of how Jesus must have looked. He had the features of love, tenderness, caring, innocence, compassion, and kindness. Arrangements were made for the young man, Pietri Bandinelli, to sit as the model for the Lord.

Years went by, and the painting still was not complete. Da Vinci could not find just the right face for Judas. He was looking for a man whose face was streaked with despair, wickedness, greed, and sin. Ten years after starting the picture, he found a man in prison whose face wore all the qualities of Judas for which he had been searching. Consent was given for the prisoner to pose, and he sat as the model for Judas.

Leonardo worked feverishly for days. But as the work went on, he noticed certain changes taking place in the prisoner. His face seemed filled with tension, and his bloodshot eyes were filled with horror as he gaped at the likeness of himself painted on the canvas. One day, Leonardo sensed

23

the man's uneasiness so greatly that he stopped painting and asked, "What seems to trouble you so much?"

The man buried his face in his hands and was convulsed with sobs. After a long time, he raised his head and inquired, "Don't you remember me? Years ago I was your model for the Lord, Jesus."

This miserable man had turned his back on Christ and turned his life over to sin and the world sucked him down to its lowest levels of degradation. He no longer loved the things he had loved before. And those things that he at one time hated and despised, now he loved. Where once there was love, now there was misery and hate; where once there was hope, now there was despair; where once there was light, now there was darkness.

And you, have you looked at your face lately?

22.
Shoes On a Goose

Anonymous

There is a story of how a farmer put shoes on a flock of geese. He was going to sell them to a poultry market in the city several miles away. However, he had no truck to get them to market, so he would have to herd them there on foot. The only road to town was surfaced with finely crushed rock, and these little rocks were sharp and would cut the webbing of the geese's feet.

Most everyone knows that the foot of a goose or a duck is shaped like a paddle. It is designed for swimming and for walking on grass or dirt, but not for walking mile upon mile over crushed rock. The farmer realized that if he herded the geese over the road, they would be limping before they got to town. If they were delivered to market in such a sorry and damaged condition, they would not fetch a high price.

He thought many days about how to overcome the

problem and finally was struck by a fantastic idea. He cleaned the floor of one of the pens and poured warm, melted road tar on it. He then shooed the geese into this pen and let them walk around long enough for the bottoms of their feet to become coated with tar. Next he lifted each goose to an adjoining pen, which was covered by clean, dry sand. As the geese waddled on the sand, the melted tar picked up a thick layer of sand as it cooled.

Wasn't that a clever way to turn obstacles into opportunities? Now each goose was equipped with a pair of road shoes. Each had an extra sole on the bottom of its feet. So off to market they went, quacking and waddling all the way, and the farmer received top price for his flock of geese that day.

23.
Let the Music Out

Anonymous

Three neighborhood boys, Salvator, Julio and Antonio, lived and played in Cremona, Italy, around the mid-1600s. Salvator had a beautiful tenor voice and Julio played the violin in accompaniment as they strolled the piazzas. Antonio also liked music and would have loved to sing along, but his voice squeaked like a creaky door hinge. All the children made fun of him whenever he tried to sing. Yet Antonio was not without talent. His most prized possession was the pocketknife his grandfather had given him. He was always whittling away on some piece of wood. In fact, Antonio made some very nice things with his whittling.

As the time for the annual festival approached, the houses and streets gradually became festooned with beautiful decorations for spring. Dressed in their finest clothes, people filled the streets. On festival day, Salvator and Julio planned to go to the cathedral where they would play and sing in the crowded plaza.

25

"Would you like to come with us?" they called to Antonio, who sat on his stoop whittling on a piece of wood. "Who cares if you can't sing. We'd like to have you come with us anyway."

"Sure, I'd like to come along," Antonio replied. "The festival is so much fun."

The three boys went off to the cathedral. As they walked along, Antonio kept thinking about their remark about his not being able to sing. It made him cry in his heart, because he loved music as much as they did, even if his voice did squeak a little.

When they arrived at the plaza, Julio began to play the violin while Salvator sang with his melodious voice. People stopped to listen, and most of them left a coin or two for the shabbily dressed boys. An elderly man stepped out from the crowd. He complimented them and placed a shiny coin into Salvator's hand. He was quickly lost in the milling crowd.

Salvator opened his hand and gasped, "Look! It's a gold coin." He clenched it between his teeth to make sure. All three boys were excited and passed the coin back and forth, examining it. They all agreed that it was a real gold piece.

"But he can well afford it," said Julio. "You know, he's the great Amati."

Antonio asked sheepishly, "And who is Amati? Why is he so great?"

Both boys laughed as they said, "You've never heard of Amati?"

"Of course he hasn't," said Julio. "He knows nothing about music makers. He has a squeaky voice and is just a whittler of wood." Julio went on, "For your information, Antonio, Amati happens to be a great violin maker, probably the best in all of Italy or even the entire world, and he even lives here in our city."

As Antonio walked home that evening, his heart was very heavy. It seemed that he had been laughed at too often for his squeaky voice and his whittling. So, very early the next morning, Antonio left his home, carrying his precious whittling knife. His pockets were stuffed with some of the things he had made—a pretty bird, a flute, several statues and a small boat. He was determined to find the home of the great Amati.

Eventually, Antonio found the house and gently knocked on the front door. When a servant opened it, the great master heard Antonio's squeaky voice and came to see what he wanted so early in the morning.

"I brought these for you to see, sir," replied Antonio, as he emptied his pockets of the assortment of items that he had carved. "I hope you will look at these and tell me if I have enough talent to learn how to make violins, too."

Amati carefully picked up and examined each piece, and invited Antonio into his house. "What is your name?" he asked.

"Antonio, sir" he squeaked.

"And why do you want to make violins," inquired Amati, now quite serious.

Impulsively Antonio blurted, "Because I love music, but I cannot sing with a voice that sounds like a squeaky door hinge. You heard how good my friends are yesterday in front of the cathedral. I, too, want to make music come alive."

Leaning forward and looking Antonio in the eyes, Amati said, "The thing that matters most is the song in the heart. There are many ways of making music—some people play the violin, others sing, still others paint wonderful pictures. Each helps to add to the splendor of the world. You are a whittler, but your song shall be as noble as any."

These words made Antonio very happy, and he never forgot this message of hope. In a very short while, Antonio became a student of the great artist. Very early, every morning, he went to Amati's workshop, where he listened and learned and watched his teacher. After many years, there was not one secret about the making of a violin, with all of its seventy different parts, that he did not know. By the time he was twenty-two years old, his master allowed him to put his own name on a violin he had made.

For the rest of his life, Antonio Stradivari made violins —more than 1,100 of them—trying to make each one better and more beautiful than the one before. Anyone who owns a Stradivarius violin owns a treasure, a masterpiece of art.

We may not be able to sing, play, whittle or make a violin, but if we really want to, we will find a way to let the music out of our hearts and to praise God with it.

24.
Walking with the Lord

David Juniper

One bright autumn morning, I was sitting at the breakfast table, thinking, "I've certainly had a lot of problems lately. Troubles at work, troubles at home, I really ought to take time to pray about them." All of a sudden, I sensed that someone had walked into the room behind me. I spun around and gasped, "Lord Jesus! What are you doing here?"

The Lord was standing in my doorway! I rubbed my eyes—was it really He? Yes, everything checked out, from the tip of the white seamless robe to the faint glimmering around his head. "That is . . . errr . . . it's not that you shouldn't be here. I'm just not used to you dropping in with such a visible form," I stammered.

This unexpected visit unsettled me. I vaguely wondered if I had done anything wrong. He smiled and the light in his eyes brightened. "Would you like to go for a walk with me?" Jesus inquired.

"Uhmmm . . . why . . . ah . . . sure!" I replied.

And so the two of us walked down the little country lane that leads past my home. Slowly, the truth began to dawn on me and I murmured to myself, "What an incredible opportunity! He has all the answers to my problems—my relationships . . . work . . . my worries about the future . . . family troubles. All I need is to ask him."

We walked quietly for several minutes, then I turned toward Him. "Excuse me, Lord," I said, "but I need some advice on a very difficult problem."

Before I could finish, Jesus raised his fingers to his lips, and tilted his head. "Shhh . . . Do you hear it?" He asked.

At first I didn't hear a thing. But then I heard the faint sound of water tumbling over rocks from a nearby stream, beneath the overhanging autumn leaves. The Lord sighed, "Isn't that beautiful?"

"Ah, yes, I suppose."

I was thoroughly distracted in my surge of thoughts. I waited a few minutes to show respect, and then blurted out, "Lord, I've been worried about my prayer life. Things have been awfully empty. Now, according to the books I've read . . ."

He put his arm around my shoulder. "Hush, do you hear it?" He asked again.

Children were playing in the nearby meadow. And again, He smiled. "Isn't it wonderful?" He exclaimed.

"Sure, now that you mention it." Then I added irritably, "You know I love children, too."

We walked on. A horrible thought loomed in my mind. What if I lost this opportunity? Here were all the answers to my troubles, right at my elbow! Jesus knew the deepest mysteries of the universe, of love, and of death. As a last resort, I decided to talk to Him about religion. After all, that is His line of work. "Lord," I ventured, "I was wondering what you think of the conflict in modern biblical scholarship between . . ."

He interrupted once more by putting a friendly arm around my shoulder, and I gritted my teeth. The Lord stopped and silently picked up several roadside pebbles. A boyish grin crossed his face. "I'll bet you can't hit the top of that telephone pole," He challenged.

I was bewildered. Why, of all things! And from the Lord himself! This was not something I expected from the Second Person of the Holy Trinity. If you were God, wouldn't you be a bit more serious about it? He casually tossed a pebble toward the pole. It arched silently through the air. Hmmm . . . Jesus missed!

My depression was deepening, but still I stooped to pick up several pebbles myself. What else could I do? Half-heartedly, I tossed it in the general direction of the pole. WHACK! I hit the pole. The Lord proudly looked at me and chuckled. "Hey you're good," He said.

As we strolled further, the knots in my stomach tightened. Whenever I wanted to talk about anything of importance, there would always be an interruption. Some faded blue chicory would be brushed by the wind, or a butterfly would light on a moss-covered fencepost.

At last our walk ended. I was so upset that I couldn't think of anything to say. Beneath His flowing black beard, the Lord had a gentle and playful smile. As He turned to leave, the light from His eyes intensified. Jesus walked to the door, glanced at me over His shoulder and said, "Just stop trying so hard."

25.
Courage or Comfort

Anonymous

Once there was a beautiful bird, more beautiful than any other. It was powerful and free, and possessed great courage. This bird was fearless, going wherever it wanted. It also was very proud of its spectacular plumage of vibrant colors.

One day the bird decided to pluck its own feathers, one by one, to make a beautiful nest in which it could rest with comfort and security. Now the bird can no longer fly.

26.
Blessing in Disguise
Anonymous

Years ago, cotton was the big money crop in the South. Then the boll weevil came along. It began eating up all the cotton crops.

Everyone despaired; ruin was imminent. However, that little pest turned out to be a blessing in disguise. It forced farmers to plant peanuts rather than cotton. Eventually peanuts became a more profitable crop than cotton ever was. In appreciation, farmers erected a statue of the hated boll weevil in Enterprise, Alabama.

27.
Liberal Arts Education
James Michener

In 1942 the U.S. Navy was desperate for talent. Four young men stood shivering in their shorts while waiting in a small room. A grim-faced selection committee asked the first would-be-officer, "What can you do?"

The recruit replied, "I'm a buyer for Macy's, and I've trained myself to judge very quickly between markets and prices and trends."

The committee replied, "Can't you do anything practical?" And they shunted him off to one side.

When the committee asked the next man, a lawyer, if he could do anything practical, he said, "I can weigh evidence and organize information." He, too, was rejected.

The third man answered the same question. "I know language and a good deal about history," he replied. The committee groaned in unison and sent him off to the side.

Then the fourth man said boldly, "I'm a college-trained engineer, and I can overhaul diesel engines." The committee wanted to make him an officer on the spot.

By the time the war was over, the Macy's buyer was assistant to the Secretary of the Navy, with many complex responsibilities requiring instant good judgment. He became an expert by taking courses in naval management and government procedures.

The lawyer wound up as assistant to Admiral Halsey, and during a critical battle he logically deduced from intelligence reports where the enemy fleet was located. He left the military bedecked with medals.

As for the third man, he got the job of naval secretary to several congressional committees and helped determine the future of American presence in the South Pacific.

And what was the fourth man, the college-trained engineer, doing at the end of the war? He was still overhauling diesel engines.

28.
A Prayer for His Son
Gen. Douglas MacArthur

Build me a son, O Lord,
>who will be strong enough to know when he is weak,
>brave enough to face himself when he is afraid . . .

Build me a son,
>whose wishes will not take the place of deeds . . .
>Lead him, I pray, not in the path of ease and comfort,
>but under the stress and spur of difficulties and
>>challenges.

Let him learn to stand in the storm;
>let him learn compassion for those who fall.

Build me a son,
>whose heart is clear, whose goals will be high;
>a son who will master himself before he seeks to master
>>others;

who will reach into the future, yet never forget the past.

And after all these things are his, add, I pray,
enough of a sense of humor
so that he may always be serious
yet never take himself too seriously . . .

Then, I, his father will dare to whisper,
"I have not lived in vain."

29.
God, Hear Me
G. Ray Funkhouser

There once was an old man who had lived a good and pious life, but in his waning years felt he had nothing to show for it. Finally, he fell to his knees and prayed, crying out: "God, hear me. I've been a good man. I've never asked anything of you before, and I'm grateful for all you have given me. So please grant me just one request, let me win the lottery."

Weeks passed and nothing happened, so he again prayed to win the lottery. Still nothing. After months of fruitless praying, he cried out to the heavens: "God, will you give me a break? All I'm asking is, let me win the lottery!"

Suddenly a voice thundered from the sky, "Will you give me a break? At least buy a ticket!"

30.
The Gift of the Magi (adapted)
O. Henry

A story is told about a young married couple whose names are Jim and Della. They are poor but very much in love with each other.

As Christmas approaches, Della wonders what to get

Jim for Christmas. She would like to give him a watch chain for his gold watch, but she doesn't have enough money. Then she gets an idea. She has beautiful long hair. So Della decides to cut off her hair and sell it to buy the fancy chain for Jim's watch.

On Christmas Eve she returns home, and in her hand is a beautiful box containing a gold watch chain which she purchased by selling her hair. Suddenly Della begins to worry. She knows Jim admired her long hair, and she wonders if he will be disappointed that she cut it off and sold it.

Della climbs the final flight of stairs leading to their tiny apartment. She unlocks the door and is surprised to find Jim home and waiting for her. In his hand is a neatly wrapped box containing his gift he purchased for her.

When Della removes her scarf Jim sees Della's short hair, and tears well up in his eyes. But he says nothing. He chokes back the tears and gives Della the gift box.

When Della opens it, she can't believe her eyes. There in the box is a set of beautiful silver combs for her long hair.

And when Jim opens his gift, he, too, is astonished. There inside the box is a beautiful gold chain for his gold pocket watch. Only then does Della realize that Jim pawned his gold watch to buy her the silver hair combs.

Far more beautiful than the gifts is the love they symbolize.

31.
The Fourth Wise Man
Henry Van Dyke

The Gospel does not tell us how many wise men, or magi, journeyed to Bethlehem following the star. Popular tradition holds that there were three—Caspar, Melchior and Balthasar. But there is also a tradition of a fourth wise man, named Artaban.

As Artaban prepared to set out and follow the star, he

took with him a sapphire, a ruby and a pearl of great price as gifts for the newborn King, wherever He is to be found.

On his way to join the other wise men, Artaban stopped to care for a sick traveler. If he stayed, however, to help he would miss the rendezvous with his friends. He stayed, and the delay was just enough to make him late for the departure of the caravan. Now Artaban was alone, and he needed transportation and supplies to cross the desert. So he sold the sapphire to purchase camels and supplies. He was saddened because the King would never have this precious gem.

Artaban journeyed onward and reached Bethlehem, but again he was too late. There were soldiers everywhere to carry out Herod's command that the male children should be slain. Artaban, therefore, took out the brilliant ruby to bribe the captain and save the children in the village in which he was staying. Children were saved, mothers rejoiced; but the ruby, also, would not reach the King.

For 33 years Artaban searched in vain, and finally found his way to Jerusalem on the day several crucifixions were to take place. Artaban hurried towards Calvary in order to bribe the Roman guard with the precious pearl and save the man called Jesus. Something told him that this was the King of Kings for whom he had been searching all his life.

Just then, a young woman being dragged along the street toward the slave market, called out to Artaban pleading for help. With only a slight hesitation, he gave the last jewel, the pearl of great price, for her ransom. Now Artaban had none of the precious gems he was going to present to the King.

Reaching the place where the crucifixions were to occur he was heartbroken when he saw that he could do nothing to help Jesus. But then something remarkable happened. Jesus looked over toward Artaban and said to him:

"Don't be brokenhearted, Artaban.
You've been helping me all your life.
When I was hungry, you gave me food,

when I was thirsty, you gave me drink,
when I was naked, you clothed me,
when I was a stranger, you took me in."

Some say Artaban never found Christ. Others say he was the wisest of the wise men.

32.
A Leader's Impact
Anonymous

In September of 1862, the Civil War tilted decisively in favor of the South. The morale of the Northern army dipped to its lowest point of the war. Large numbers of Union troops were in full retreat in Virginia. Northern leaders began to fear the worst. They saw no way to reverse the situation and turn the beaten, exhausted troops into a useful army again.

There was only one general with the ability to work such a miracle. That was General George McClellan. He had trained the men for combat and they admired him. But neither the War Department nor the rest of the Cabinet members saw this connection. Only President Abraham Lincoln recognized Gen. McClellan's leadership skills.

Fortunately, Lincoln ignored the protests of his advisors and reinstated McClellan back in command. He told the general to go down to Virginia and give those soldiers something no other man on earth could give them: enthusiasm, strength and hope. McClellan accepted the command. He mounted his great black horse and cantered down the dusty Virginia roads.

What happened next is hard to describe. Northern leaders couldn't explain it. Union soldiers couldn't explain it either. Even McClellan couldn't quite explain what happened. Gen. McClellan met the retreating Union columns, waved his cap in the air and shouted words of encouragement. When the worn out men saw their beloved teacher and leader, they began to take heart once again. They were moved with an unshakable feeling that now things could be different, that finally things could be all right again.

Bruce Catton, the great Civil War historian, describes this excitement that grew when word spread that McClellan was back in command. "Down mile after mile of Virginia roads the stumbling columns came alive. Men threw their caps and knapsacks into the air, and yelled until they could yell no more . . . because they saw this dapper little rider outlined against the purple starlight.

"And this, in a way, was the turning point of the war. . . . No one could ever quite explain how it happened. But whatever it was, it gave President Lincoln and the North what was needed. And history was forever changed because of it."

The story of Gen. McClellan illustrates dramatically the impact a leader can have on the human spirit.

33.
Need to Ask Others
Anonymous

One day a small boy was trying to lift a heavy stone, but he couldn't budge it. His father, passing by, stopped to watch his son's efforts. Finally he said to his son: "Are you using all your strength?"

Exasperated, the boy cried, "Yes, I am."

"No you're not," said the father calmly. "You haven't asked me to help you."

34.
The Lion and the Bull
Anonymous

A hungry mountain lion came out of the hills to stalk a grazing herd. The lion attacked a bull and killed it. As it feasted on its kill, the lion paused from time to time to let out a scream in triumph.

A hunter, who was in the area, heard the commotion, found the mountain lion and shot it dead.

The moral of this story: When you're full of bull, keep your mouth shut.

35.
Know the Shepherd
Anonymous

After a large dinner at one of Hollywood's stately mansions, a famous actor entertained the guests with stunning readings of Shakespeare. Then, as an encore, he offered to accept a request. A shy, older priest asked if he knew Psalm 23. The actor said, "Yes, I do and I will give it on one condition: that when I am finished you recite the very same psalm."

The priest was a little bit embarrassed, but consented. The actor did a beautiful rendition . . . "My shepherd is the Lord, there is nothing I shall want . . ." The guests applauded loudly when the actor finished, and then it was the priest's turn. He got up and said the same words, but this time there was no applause, just a hushed silence and the beginnings of a tear in several eyes.

The actor savored the silence for a few moments and then stood up. "Ladies and gentlemen," he said, "I hope you realize what happened here tonight. I knew the words to the psalm, but this priest knows the Shepherd."

36.
Bravery? . . . New Brakes!
Mike Wickett

Many years ago there was a huge oil refinery fire. Flames shot hundreds of feet into the air. The sky was thick with grimy, black smoke. The heat was intense—so intense that firefighters had to park their trucks a block away and wait for the heat to die down before they could begin to fight the fire. However, it was about to rage out of control.

Then all of a sudden, from several blocks away came a fire truck, racing down the street with its brakes screeching. It hit the curb in front of the fire. The firefighters jumped out and began to battle the blaze. All the firefighters who were parked a block away saw this, and they jumped into their trucks, drove down the block and began to fight the fire, too. As a result of that cooperative effort, they were just barely able to bring the fire under control.

The people who saw this teamwork thought, "My goodness, the man who drove that lead fire truck—what an act of bravery!" They decided to give him a special award to recognize him for his bravery in leading the charge.

At the ceremony the mayor said, "Captain, we want to honor you for a fantastic act of bravery. You prevented the loss of property—perhaps even the loss of life. If there is one special thing you could have—just about anything—what would it be?"

Without hesitation, the captain replied, "Your Honor, a new set of brakes would be dandy!"

37.
Don't Rest on Laurels

Anonymous

One day a field marshal requested an audience with Napoleon, and Napoleon knew what was coming. But as every good leader must, Napoleon agreed to hear him out. The field marshal brought news of a great victory he had achieved. He talked for a long time about his accomplishment, piling detail upon detail.

Napoleon listened closely throughout the entire narration, but said nothing. The officer was disappointed. He had hoped for a more enthusiastic reception, as well as Napoleon's congratulations. Neither was forthcoming.

Summing up, the marshal repeated much of what he had already stated. As the officer rambled on, Napoleon continued to listen politely, and the marshal interpreted this as encouragement. Surely, he thought, Napoleon will now give me the praise I so richly deserve.

When the marshal finally stopped talking, Napoleon asked him one question: "What did you do the next day?"

The field marshal was speechless. But the lesson was not lost on him. From then on, the officer understood that he should never rest on his laurels. So he left it to others to bestow the praise.

38.
The Great Stone Face

Nathaniel Hawthorne

In a pleasant, sunny valley surrounded by lofty mountains, lived a boy name Ernest. On the side of one of the mountains, in bold relief, nature had carved the features of a gigantic face.

From the steps of his cottage, the boy used to gaze intently upon the stone face, for his mother had told him that some day a man would come to the valley who would look just like the Great Stone Face. His coming would bring joy and happiness to the entire community.

"Mother," said the boy, "I wish that it could speak, for it looks so kind that its voice must be pleasant. If I were to see a man with such a face, I should love him dearly." So, Ernest continued to gaze at the Great Stone Face for hours at a time.

Several times the rumor spread that the long-looked-for benefactor was coming, but each time when the man arrived, the rumor proved to be false. In the meantime, Ernest had grown into manhood, doing good wherever he could. The people in the village loved him. Everyone was his friend. And as he became an old man, Ernest was still looking for the arrival of the long-expected one.

One day a poet came into the valley. He had heard the prophecy about the Great Stone Face, and at evening, when the sun was setting, he saw Ernest talking to some people. As the last rays of light flooded the massive outlines on the distant mountainside, they fell on Ernest's face. The poet cried aloud, "Behold! Behold! Ernest himself is the likeness of the Great Stone Face."

Then all the people looked, and sure enough, they saw that what the poet said was true. By looking daily at the Great Stone Face, Ernest had become like it.

If we gaze intently on Jesus as our Teacher and Example, we will become more like Him.

39.
Transformation to New Life (adapted)

Cecil B. De Mille

"What a great afternoon this is," thought the young boy. "Grandpa and me fishing all by ourselves." The two of them just talked and fished, and aimlessly drifted in a rowboat on a lake. The boy became restless—normal for a boy —and he leaned over the side to look into the water. There, just beneath the surface, a bunch of water beetles were flitting around as if they were playing.

Suddenly one of the water beetles crawled up on an oar. When it got halfway up, it attached the talons of its legs to the wooden oar and died. The boy's curiosity was aroused and he interrupted his grandfather's nap to show him. They went back to fishing.

About three hours later, the boy looked down at the

dead beetle. What he saw caused him to jump, almost tipping the boat. The beetle had dried up, and its shell started to crack open. Both the astonished grandfather and the boy watched silently at what unfolded before their eyes.

Something began to emerge from the opening: first long tentacles, then a head, then moist wings until, finally, a beautiful dragonfly fully emerged.

They both stared in awe. The dragonfly began to move its wings, slowly at first. Then it hovered gracefully over the water where the other water beetles were still flitting around. They didn't even recognize the dragonfly. They didn't realize that it was the same beetle they had played with some three hours earlier.

The boy took his finger and nudged the dried-out shell of the beetle. It was like an empty tomb.

40.
Become What You Want to Be

Anonymous

Let me tell you about a little girl who was born into a very poor family in a shack in the backwoods of Tennessee. She was the 20th of 22 children, prematurely born and frail. Her survival was doubtful. When she was four years old she had double pneumonia and scarlet fever—a deadly combination that left her with a paralyzed and useless left leg. She had to wear an iron leg brace. Yet she was fortunate in having a mother who encouraged her.

Well, this mother told her little girl, who was very bright, that despite the brace and leg, she could do whatever she wanted to do with her life. She told her that all she needed to do was to have faith, persistence, courage and an indomitable spirit.

So at nine years of age, the little girl removed the leg brace, and she took the step the doctors told her she would never take normally. In four years, she developed a rhythmic stride, which was a medical wonder. Then this girl got the notion, the incredible notion, that she would like to be the world's greatest woman runner. Now, what could she mean —be a runner with a leg like that?

At age 13, she entered a race. She came in last—way, way last. She entered every race in high school, and in every race she came in last. Everyone begged her to quit! However, one day, she came in next to last. And then there came a day when she won a race. From then on, Wilma Rudolph won every race that she entered.

Wilma went to Tennessee State University, where she met a coach named Ed Temple. Coach Temple saw the indomitable spirit of the girl, that she was a believer and that she had great natural talent. He trained her so well that she went to the Olympic Games.

There she was pitted against the greatest woman runner of the day, a German girl named Jutta Heine. Nobody had ever beaten Jutta. But in the 100-meter dash, Wilma Rudolph won. She beat Jutta again in the 200-meters. Now Wilma had two Olympic gold medals.

Finally came the 400-meter relay. It would be Wilma against Jutta once again. The first two runners on Wilma's team made perfect handoffs with the baton. But when the third runner handed the baton to Wilma, she was so excited she dropped it, and Wilma saw Jutta taking off down the track. It was impossible that anybody could catch this fleet and nimble girl. But Wilma did just that! Wilma Rudolph had earned three Olympic gold medals.

41.
Life Is a Struggle

Anonymous

A student found a cocoon one day and brought it to his homeroom which was in the biology lab. The teacher put it into an unused aquarium with a lamp to keep the cocoon warm. About a week went by when a small opening began to appear on the underside of the cocoon. The students watched as it began to shake. Suddenly, tiny antennae emerged, followed by the head and tiny front feet. The students would run back to the lab in between classes to check on the progress of the cocoon. By lunchtime it had struggled to free its listless wings, the colors revealing that it was a monarch butterfly. It wiggled, shook, and struggled, but now it seemed to be stuck. Try as it might, the butterfly couldn't seem to force its body through the small opening in the cocoon.

Finally, one student decided to help the butterfly out of its difficulty. He took scissors from the table, snipped off the cocoon's restrictive covering, and out plopped an insect-like thing. The top half looked like a butterfly with droopy wings, the bottom half, which was just out of the cocoon, was large and swollen. The butter-pillar or cater-fly never flew with its stunted wings. It just crawled around the bottom of the aquarium dragging its wings and swollen body. Within a short time it died.

The next day the biology teacher explained that the butterfly's struggle to get through the tiny opening was necessary in order to force the fluids from the swollen body into the wings so that they would be strong enough to fly. Without the struggle the wings never developed and the butterfly could not fly.

As for the butterfly, so too for us—we cannot violate the Laws of Creation. Without struggles a lot of things in life never develop.

42.
Map Makers and Dragons
Roger Von Oech

Centuries ago, when map makers ran out of the known world before they ran out of parchment, they would sketch a

44

dragon at the edge of the scroll. This was a sign to the explorer that he would be entering unknown territory at his own risk. Unfortunately, some explorers took this symbol literally and were afraid to push on to new worlds. Other more adventuresome explorers saw the dragon as a sign of opportunity, a door to new territory.

Each person has a mental map that contains the information we use to guide ourselves in our day-to-day encounters. Like the maps of long ago, our mental maps also have dragons on them. Sometimes these dragons are valid warnings. Other times, however, they prevent us from discovering something new.

43.
Excuses

Theophane the Monk

A middle-aged woman went to a distant monastery for her first weekend retreat in many years. When she arrived at the guest house one of the monks approached her and surprised her with a brusque question, "Why not?"

"That was the first thing he said," she relates. "He had never seen me before. I hadn't even said a word. 'Why not?' he questioned. I knew he had me. After all, he was the retreat master."

I brought up excuses: "It was a long trip . . . I'm tired . . . the kids . . . the people I have to work with . . . not enough time . . . I guess it's my temperament."

The retreat master took a long sword off the wall and gave it to the woman. "Here, with this sword, you can cut through any barriers you have." She took it and slipped away without saying another word.

Back in her room, alone, she sat down and kept looking at that sword. She knew that what he said was true. But the next day she returned the sword. She muttered, "How can I live without my excuses."

44.
Refining Gold

Anonymous

Near Cripple Creek, Colorado, gold and tellurium occur mixed as tellurite ore. The refining methods of the early mining camps could not separate the two elements, so the ore was thrown into a scrap heap.

One day a miner mistook a lump of ore for coal and tossed it into his stove. Later, while removing ashes from the stove, he found the bottom littered with beads of pure gold. The heat had burned away the tellurium, leaving the gold in a purified state. The discarded ore was reworked and yielded a fortune.

People are like tellurite ore. We have gold inside us, but it often takes some trial in the fiery furnace of life to transform us.

45.
The Missionary's Sundial

Anonymous

Years ago a missionary who worked in a rural part of Brazil returned home to America for a holiday. While he was home, he happened to come across a beautiful sundial. Immediately he got an idea. "That sundial would be an ideal gift for my villagers up the Amazon River," he thought. "I could use it to teach them how to tell the time of the day."

The missionary bought the sundial, crated it up, and took it back to the interior of Brazil. When the village leader saw it, he insisted that it be set up in the center of the village.

The villagers also were thrilled with the sundial. They had never seen anything so beautiful in their lives. They were even more excited when they learned how it worked.

The missionary was delighted by everyone's response to

the sundial. He was therefore totally unprepared for what happened a few days later. The people of the village got together and built a roof over the sundial to protect it from the rain and the sun.

46.
Desire Does Make a Difference

Zig Ziglar

The topic of desire reminds me of a story about a baseball player who back in 1945 played for the St. Louis Browns. Now the Browns were arguably the weakest major league team ever to take the field. Their won-lost record was three shades worse than pathetic.

They had a player who lasted only one year. He was an outfielder. He was not even a regular and he never got a home run. Yet this player has to qualify as a legitimate candidate for the Hall of Fame. The young man's name was Pete Gray.

As a young man, Gray had a burning desire, an absolutely overwhelming ambition, and that ambition was to play major league baseball. And he did it, despite the fact that he had only one arm. However, that one arm, coupled with a tremendous desire, enabled Pete Gray to get all the way to the major leagues. So many times, desire is the thing that does make a difference.

47.
A Sermon Walking

Anonymous

One afternoon in 1953, reporters and officials gathered at a Chicago railroad station to await the arrival of the 1952 Nobel Peace Prize winner. He stepped off the train—a giant of a man, six-feet-four, with bushy hair and a large moustache.

As cameras flashed, city officials approached with hands outstretched and began telling him how honored they were to meet him. He thanked them politely and then, looking over their heads, asked if he could be excused for a moment. He walked through the crowd with quick strides until he reached the side of an elderly black woman who was struggling as she tried to carry two large suitcases.

He picked up the bags in his big hands and, smiling, escorted the woman to a bus. As he helped her aboard, he wished her a safe journey. Meanwhile, the crowd tagged along behind him. He turned to them and said, "Sorry to have kept you waiting."

The man was Dr. Albert Schweitzer, the famous missionary-doctor, who had spent his life helping the poorest of the poor in Africa. A member of the reception committee said to one of the reporters: "That's the first time I ever saw a sermon walking."

48.
The Conceited Scholar

Gautama Buddha

Once upon a time an old wise man lived the life of a village merchant. One day a learned scholar came to the village. While strutting along, the scholar, who was a very conceited man, came upon a place where a large ram was standing about. Seeing the scholar approach, the ram bent his horns low to the ground and stepped back, preparing to charge.

The scholar, rapt in his conceit, fancied to himself, "It is this ram, above all others in this world who truly understands my greatness. For this reason the beast humbly bows before me." Thinking in this manner the scholar composed a verse:

The kindly beast obeisance makes before
The high caste brahmin in holy lore.
Good honest creature thou,
Famous above all others beasts, I vow!

Sitting nearby, the wise and noble merchant tried to warn the scholar. He spoke another verse:

Brahmin, be not so foolish this beast to trust,
Or else he will lay you in the dust.
It is for this reason which the ram falls back
To gain an impetus for his attack!

The merchant had barely finished speaking when the ram charged forward, striking the haughty scholar on his thigh sending him flying into the air. Landing face down in the dust, the scholar felt great pain and humiliation. To explain what had happened to the people gathered around, the merchant rejoined with another verse:

With broken leg and pride upset,
His damaged fortune will he sore regret.
Let him not weep with outstretched arms in vain,
Haste to the rescue before the scholar is slain!

Shaken to his senses, the scholar came back with this verse:

Thus all those who desire honor, I say,
Will share the same fate that I have met today.
Knocked in the dust by a butting ram laid low,
It is but to foolish conceit that my fate I owe!

49.
Hidden Capacities
Alan McGinnis

History books are full of stories of gifted persons whose talents were overlooked by a procession of people until someone believed in them. Albert Einstein was four years old before he could speak and seven before he could read. Isaac Newton did poorly in grade school. A newspaper editor fired Walt Disney because he had "no good ideas." Wernher von Braun failed ninth grade algebra. Joseph Haydn gave up on making a musician out of Beethoven, who seemed a slow and plodding man with no apparent talent.

There is a lesson in such stories: different people develop at different rates, and the best motivators are always on the lookout for hidden capacities.

50.
The Power of the Resurrection

Fr. Leonard, S.T.

Last week, the Resurrection took on another new meaning for me. It was a particularly hectic week. I felt as if I were running from pillar-to-post starting fires in some places and putting them out in others. The last thing I wanted to hear at the end of the day on Friday was that I had a visitor.

Before I had a chance to respond to the announcement, a young woman appeared at my door and asked if we could talk. My voice responded, "Certainly," but my heart begged her to let me finish clearing off my desk.

It is not with any sense of pride that I tell you that I didn't clear off my desk, but rather sat down to talk with and listen to this stranger who really needed help. Her story was long and it was heartbreaking. And when I realized how much more difficult it was to tell than to listen, I forgot what chores I had left undone, and listened with my whole heart and soul.

That young woman left my office many hours later, still carrying with her the same problems that she had brought in. But she also left knowing that she was not alone and that someone thought she was important enough to hear her out.

For my part, I was reminded that one of the messages of the Resurrection is that we are never alone. I learned that when we make ourselves consciously present to others, when we pay attention to them—we resurrect them—we give them new life, just as Jesus gave it to you and to me.

51.
A Hero's Compassion
Bob Greene

Bob Greene, a columnist for the *Chicago Tribune*, relates that one cold night after a game, Chicago Bulls superstar Michael Jordan, headed through a large crowd of fans toward his car. As he opened the car door, Jordan saw a youngster in a wheelchair some 20 feet away. The boy's neck was bent at an unnatural angle; his eyes could not look directly forward. Jordan walked over to the boy and knelt beside him. The youngster was so excited that he began to rise out of the wheelchair. Michael comforted him, talked softly, and put his arm around the boy's frail shoulder.

The boy's father tried to snap a picture, but the camera didn't work. Jordan noticed. Without being asked, he continued to kneel at the boy's side until the father was able to take the picture. Only then did Michael return to his car.

The boy's eyes were glistening with tears of joy. His dad was already replaying the moment with his son. If nothing good ever happens again for that little boy, he will always know that on one night Michael Jordan cared enough to include him in his world.

52.
Cooperation of Two Mules
Anonymous

A farmer once took two stubborn mules and tied them together by a 20-foot length of rope. Two bales of hay lay on the ground, one at either end of the field. The animals kept straining and tugging against each other, each trying to get to the bale of hay nearest it. Finally, they both collapsed and died of starvation.

Are there any mules in your world?

53.
Reach Out or Pass By

Anonymous

A woman was standing on a curb, waiting for the traffic light to change. On the opposite curb was a girl about 17 years old. The woman noticed that the girl was crying.

When the light changed, each started across the street. Just as they were about to meet, the woman's motherly instincts came rushing to the surface. Every part of her wanted to reach out and comfort that girl. But the woman passed her by. She didn't even greet her; she just kept going.

Hours later the tear-filled eyes of that girl continued to haunt the woman. Over and over she said to herself, "Why didn't I turn to her and say, 'Can I be of help?' Sure she might have rejected me, but so what! Only a few seconds would have been enough to let her know that someone cared for her. Instead, I passed on by. I acted as if she didn't exist."

54.
Need to Win

Thomas Merton

When archers are shooting for practice, they possess all their skill. If they shoot for a brass buckle, they are already nervous. If they shoot for a prize of gold, they go blind or they see two targets—they are out of their minds!

Their skill has not changed, but the prize divides them.

They care, care too much. They think more of winning than of shooting arrows—and the need to win drains them of power.

55.
Life Is Like a Cafeteria

Anonymous

A friend's grandfather came to America from Eastern Europe. After being processed at Ellis Island, he went into a cafeteria in lower Manhattan to get something to eat. He sat down at an empty table and waited for someone to take his order. Of course nobody did. Finally, a woman with a tray full of food sat down opposite him and informed him how a cafeteria worked.

"Start out at that end," she said. "Just go along the line and pick out what you want. At the other end they'll tell you how much you have to pay."

"I soon learned that's how everything works in America," the grandfather told a friend. "Life's a cafeteria here. You can get anything you want as long as you are willing to pay the price. You can even get success, but you'll never get it if you wait for someone to bring it to you. You have to get up and get it yourself."

56.
How to Catch Monkeys

Anonymous

Have you heard the story about how some people in India catch monkeys?

They cut a small hole in a sturdy box; then they put a tasty nut inside the box. The hole is just large enough for the monkey to put its hand through, but it's too small for the monkey to withdraw its hand once it has clutched the nut inside.

So the monkey has two choices. It can let go of the nut and go free, or it can clutch the nut and remain trapped. Monkeys usually hang onto the nut.

What do you hang on to? As long as you hang on, you cannot go free. And you remain trapped.

57.
Sitting This One Out
Anonymous

During the late 1960s, a couple was traveling around California. One day they noticed a pleasant-appearing young man sitting by a bridge near their hotel. They saw him sitting in that same spot day after day. Finally, becoming curious, they asked him why he sat in that one spot all day, every day. He told them, "I happen to believe in reincarnation. I believe that I have lived many times before and that I will have many lives following this one. So this life I'm sitting out."

So, what's your reason, your excuse for just sitting there?

58.
Sparky—Charlie Brown
Earl Nightingale

A story is told about a boy named Sparky. For Sparky school was all but impossible. He failed every subject in the eighth grade. He flunked physics in high school. Receiving a flat zero in the course, he distinguished himself as the worst physics student in the school's history. Sparky also flunked Latin, algebra and English. He didn't do much better in sports. Although he did manage to make the school's golf team, he promptly lost the only important match of the season. There was a consolation match; he lost that, too.

Throughout his youth Sparky was awkward socially. He was not actually disliked by the other students; no one cared that much. He was astonished if a classmate ever said hello to him outside of school hours. There's no way to tell how he might have done at dating. Sparky never once asked a girl to go out in high school. He was too afraid of being turned down.

Sparky was a loser. He, his classmates . . . everyone knew it. So he rolled with it. Sparky had made up his mind early in life that if things were meant to work out, they would. Otherwise he would content himself with what appeared to be his inevitable mediocrity.

However, one thing *was* important to Sparky—drawing. He was proud of his artwork. Of course, no one else appreciated it. In his senior year of high school, he submitted some cartoons to the editors of the yearbook. They were turned down. Despite this particularly painful rejection, Sparky was so convinced of his ability that he decided to become a professional artist.

Upon graduating from high school, he wrote a letter to Walt Disney Studios. He was told to send some samples of his artwork, and the subject matter for a cartoon was suggested. Sparky drew the proposed cartoon. He spent a great deal of time on it and on all the other drawings he submitted. Finally the reply came from Disney Studios, he had been rejected once again. Another loss for the loser.

So Sparky decided to write his own autobiography in cartoons. He described his childhood self—a little-boy loser and chronic underachiever. The cartoon character would soon become famous worldwide. For Sparky, the boy who had failed every subject in the eighth grade and whose work was rejected again and again, was Charles Schulz. He created the "Peanuts" comic strip and the little cartoon boy whose kite would never fly and who never succeeded in kicking the football—Charlie Brown.

59.
The Monk's Vision

Lawrence Le Shan

An old monk prayed many years for a vision from God to strengthen his faith, but it never came. He had almost given up hope when, one day, a vision appeared. The old monk was overjoyed. But then, right in the middle of the vision, the monastery bell rang. The ringing of the bell meant it was time to feed the poor who gathered daily at the monastery gate. And it was the old monk's turn to feed them. If he failed to show up with food, the poor people would leave quietly, thinking the monastery had nothing to give them that day.

The old monk was torn between his earthly duty and his heavenly vision. However, before the bell stopped tolling, the monk had made his decision. With a heavy heart, he turned his back on the vision and went off to feed the poor. Nearly an hour later, the old monk returned to his room. When he opened the door, he could hardly believe his eyes. There in the room was the vision, waiting for him. As the monk dropped to his knees in thanksgiving, the vision said to him, "My son, had you not gone off to feed the poor, I would not have stayed."

The best way to serve God is to reach out in service to our brothers and sisters, especially those less gifted than ourselves.

60.
Secret of Happiness

Anonymous

There's an old legend about a tribe that was always at war with other tribes. They murdered, raped and pillaged.

They had no morals, love, or compassion. They were so violent, they seemed to have a death wish.

An alarmed elder called together some reasonable members from all the other tribes to try and save the violent tribe's people from themselves. After much discussion the reasonable people decided to take the secret of success and happiness away from those who abused it and hide it from them.

But where should this secret be hidden? Some suggested it be buried deep in the earth. Others said to put it on top of the highest mountain. Still others suggested it be sunk deep in the ocean. There was no agreement until the elder who had gathered them together made this proposal. "Let us hide the secret within the people themselves," he suggested. "People like this will never find happiness and success there."

To this day people have been feverishly pursuing success and happiness, searching for the secret. Relatively few ever find its hiding place—already within themselves.

61.
The Little Guy with a Big Dream

Donna Menis

Mike Iuzzolino, better known as Izz, is a young man who lives to play basketball. At just 13 years old he made the decision to quit playing other sports and to concentrate all his energies on playing basketball.

At an early age Mike developed the discipline to practice, practice, practice. It was not uncommon to see him dribbling a basketball while carrying his books. This self-discipline eventually evolved into a daily workout ritual. Every morning before school he lifted weights and shot 100 free throws. Every afternoon before practice he tossed 100 jump shots. During the summer, he often played long into the evening on a court in the alley next to his house, using the streetlight to see the hoop.

He became a standout point guard at Altoona High School in Pennsylvania, and won all-state honors his senior year.

Despite his outstanding shooting ability, Mike didn't attract the attention of very many major college basketball programs. You see, Izz was only five-feet, ten-inches tall, trying to make it in a "big" man's game. Penn State did offer him a scholarship, however, and Mike grabbed at the chance to continue playing ball at the college level.

During his freshman and sophomore years at Penn State, Mike spent most of his time on the bench, and averaged only 2.8 points a game. He was frustrated, but not discouraged. He continued his personal practice rituals. When he wasn't practicing, he was studying. He became an honor student.

At the end of his sophomore year, Mike decided to leave Penn State. He wanted to play the game he loved; however, it looked like he wouldn't be getting much "PT" (play time) at Penn State.

He transferred to Saint Francis College, a small liberal arts college in Loretto, PA, only 30 minutes from his home. He could not play basketball his first year at Saint Francis because of NCAA transfer regulations, but he did continue his personal daily practice. Once again Mike Iuzzolino was on the bench watching others play the game he loved.

When his chance did come the next year, Mike made the most of it. He averaged 21 points per game his junior season and 24 his senior year. Izz finished among the nation's leaders in three major scoring categories, making him the best all-around shooter in the country. Mike was named "Player of the Year" in the Northeast Conference and "Most Valuable Player" of the conference tournament.

Mike won in the classroom as well. He was twice named a first team Academic All-American. Mike also was recognized as the Mercedes-Benz Scholar-Athlete of the Year and "Champions" Scholar-Athlete, earning him scholarships for graduate school.

Mike's lifelong dream of making it to the NCAA tournament became a reality on a March evening in Loretto, when Saint Francis' Red Flash team defeated a heavily favored Fordham squad to win the first ever NCAA play-in game and gain a berth as one of 64 teams in the annual "March Madness" tournament.

For most people, what Mike Iuzzolino had overcome —lack of height, lack of playing time, lack of national media attention—was a lifetime's worth of adversity. Now Izz could enjoy what he had persevered so hard to accomplish.

However, Mike had one more dream—the most fantastic one of all. He wanted to play in the National Basketball Association. Never mind that only two percent of all college players ever make it to the NBA. Never mind that, as one sportscaster put it, "Five-foot, ten-inch guys aren't supposed to be drafted by the NBA."

Don't tell that to Mike. Taking advantage of the opportunity to demonstrate his deadly three-point shooting accuracy during pre-draft camps, Izz won over all doubters and showed that he could play with the big guys. On June 26, 1991, in the NBA draft, Mike Iuzzolino was the 35th pick, a second round choice of the Dallas Mavericks.

The axiom still holds . . . most little guys don't stand a chance of making it to the NBA. But little guys with big dreams who possess courage and determination do make it.

62.
Power of Compassion

Fr. Jim McNamara

The young minister walked slowly to the office, mumbling to himself that he was not "on call" that day, and that it was almost supper time. There in the office sat a young man. His clothes and the emanating stench told the minister that here was a street-person who had not bathed lately. He introduced himself only as "Jim." As Jim began his story, he mentioned that he had no place to stay.

The minister could see it coming. He was going to ask for money. Deep inside himself he was hoping that the housekeeper would interrupt and call him to dinner. The young man continued his sad story. To the minister it dragged slowly on. Then the housekeeper knocked on the office door to tell the minister that he was wanted on the phone. He excused himself and went to answer the phone.

When he returned, the minister found that Jim had left. The minister sensed that his manner had revealed his preoccupation with other things. So he looked outside, up and down the street, but could not see his departed visitor. Feeling the growing twinges of remorse, he got into his car and drove through the neighborhood.

Finally, he spotted Jim and pulled his car up to the curb. When he called out to Jim, there was no answer. The poor fellow just kept on walking. So the minister parked the car, ran up the sidewalk, and stood in front of the young man, "Jim, I'm sorry that I had to leave. Would you come back with me and finish our conversation?"

The young man simply shrugged and said in a low whisper, "You're just like everybody else. No one wants to listen." With that Jim walked around the minister and disappeared into the night.

63.
The Frog Prince
David K. Reynolds, Ph.D.

Once upon a time there was a prince who had been turned into a frog. The transition wasn't instantaneous as is the fate of most fairy tale prince-frogs. In this case the process was gradual, over thirty years or so. You would think that a gradual change might be less traumatic than a sudden transformation; after all, the royal fellow had had a chance to adjust to his amphibious state. In a way, however, the slow change was even worse. The inevitability of the final result ate away at the prince's mind. Day by day he noticed that his voice was changing, warts were appearing, his skin color was becoming gray-green, his eyes and feet and back were becoming more frog-like, and he was shrinking in size.

That's not an experience likely to produce gusto in a prince. "What's happening to me? What witch have I offended to produce this spell of hoppitis?" he wondered.

The prince spent a few years flitting around the land collecting kisses from princesses before he turned completely "froginous" and ugly. After all, he had read the fairy tales about the magic antidote of a maiden's kiss. Unfortunately, the virus strain that he suffered from didn't respond to the magic of that old child's tale. Eventually, he gave up and accepted his gradual transformation.

To make a long "tale" short, by age sixty the prince was a complete frog, hopping along, minding his diet, completely resigned to his fate.

He fell in love with an elderly lady frog, and, upon kissing her warty, fly-specked face, he found that he was instantly changed into a prince again. Well, at least for a moment. From then on, for varying periods of time after kissing her, he felt as if he were a prince and she were a princess. How about that!

Princes grow old; that is, if they live long enough, all princes become frogs.

64.
Names in the Bible
Anonymous

The parish Bible study group was studying personalities of the Bible. In the study guide they were asked to tell who they would like to be.

One woman said, "Ruth." Another, "Mary." An older man said, "King Solomon." A young man replied, "Paul." A young woman chimed in saying, "I would like to be Lo."

Everyone was puzzled, not recalling anyone named Lo in the Bible. They quizzed her on the passage. She said, "Lo, I am with you always."

65.
Validity of Religions

Anonymous

Down at the local coffee shop two farmers were arguing about the validity of their respective religions. A third farmer listened for a while and then observed out loud, "I's been bringin' my wheat here to this same mill for over 40 years. Now, there be two roads that lead up to the mill. Never once, friends, has the miller asked me which road I takes. He just asks, 'Is your wheat good?' "

66.
No Time to Brag

Mongolian Folklore

Two geese were about to start southward on their annual migration, when they were entreated by a frog to take him with them. The geese expressed their willingness to do so if a means of conveyance could be devised.

The frog produced a long stalk of pond grass, got the geese each to grab an end with their beaks, while he clung to it by his mouth in the middle. In this way the three began their journey. Some farmers below noticed the strange sight. The men loudly expressed their admiration for the travel device and wondered who had been clever enough to discover it. Whereupon the vainglorious frog opened his mouth to say, "It was I," lost his grip, fell to the earth and was dashed to pieces.

Moral: When you have a good thing going, keep your mouth shut!

67.
Logic and Thinking

Anonymous

A philosophy professor at the university was trying to explain to the class what a course in logic could do for a person's thinking. "Suppose," he said, "that two people came out of a chimney. One is clean and one is dirty. Which one takes a bath?" asked the professor.

"The dirty one, naturally," answered a student.

The professor pointed out, "Remember, the clean person sees the dirty one and notices how dirty he is and vice versa. Now, which one takes a bath?"

"I get it now," answered another student. "The clean chimney sweep sees the dirty one and concludes that he's dirty, too—so he takes a bath. Am I correct?"

"Wrong. Absolutely wrong," said the professor. "Logic teaches you that if two workers go into a chimney, how could one come out clean and another one dirty?"

68.
New Creatures in Christ

Anonymous

Queen Victoria once paid a visit to a paper mill. Without knowing who this distinguished visitor was, the foreman showed her the workings of the mill. She went into the rag-sorting shop where employees picked out the rags from the refuse of the city. Upon inquiring what was done with this dirty mass of rags, she was told that it would eventually make the finest white writing paper. After her departure, the foreman found out who it was that had paid the visit.

Some time later, Her Majesty received a package of the most delicate, pure white stationery, bearing the Queen's likeness for a watermark. Enclosed was a note saying that the stationery had been made from the dirty rags she had recently inspected.

This story illustrates Christ's work in us, as well. He takes us, filthy as we are, and makes us into new creatures. After receiving Jesus, we are as spiritually different from what we were before, as pure white paper is from the filthy rags from which it is made.

69.
The Care-Collector

Leo Remington

In a bustling village, somewhere and sometime, there was a town square surrounded by trees where the collectors gathered. These were people who made a living collecting things other people had discarded. The collectors discovered that once you had enough of various discarded items, they became valuable again. The people of the village had the notion that if something was for sale, it must be worth buying. However strange this may seem, it was what the people thought, and this notion served the collectors well.

One collector had a splendid supply of glass bottles. He attracted attention to them by hanging some from a tree and clinking them with sticks to make music. Another collector had a cartload of odd-sized shoes. She often commented how odd in size and shape people's feet were, so sooner or later her odd assortment of shoes would be distributed to the appropriate feet.

There were pot and pan collectors, stamp and book collectors, golf club and hat collectors, and comic book and sports card collectors. All in all, it was quite a collection of collectors.

One day an old man came wandering into the village asking where the collectors' plaza was located. He carried a large pack, but didn't seem to be burdened by its weight. Eventually, he found the square where the collectors collected, and he established himself off in one corner.

Naturally, the collectors discovered there was a new collector in town, and they eagerly inquired about what he had in the pack. He simply told them there was nothing in it but his lunch and a raincoat in case it rained. "You mean, you don't have a collection of some kind?" they asked. "Aren't you a collector?"

"Oh, yes," he said, "I'm very much a collector. But what I collect does not fit in a pack or a box. I collect people's cares."

This was a strange idea to the people who heard this, so they asked him to explain. "Well, you see, I discovered long ago that one of the things everybody has too many of and constantly tries to get rid of, are cares, trials, burdens, sorrows, difficult times—all kinds of things that weigh them down and make their lives sad. So I offer to collect these cares from the people and they feel better. Isn't that simple?"

Some of the regular collectors who heard this thought it was a silly belief and possibly one that was dangerous to their honored profession. They even considered reporting him to the collector inspector.

The old man didn't seem to harm anyone, though, so they left him alone. Soon enough, someone asked him how he collected cares, and he replied, "Well, there is probably something in your life that bothers you right now—some care that you have. Just tell me about it and I will add it to my collection."

"But how will that help me?" the inquirer asked. "Can you make the problem go away just because I tell you about it?"

"No," the care-collector replied, "but you will feel better about it. Try it."

So the person told the old man about something that was a problem. When the story was finished, the care-collector nodded his head deeply a few times, and then put his hands together as if to scoop up something heavy. He pretended to put it into his pack. "There, I have put it away. How do you feel?" he asked.

The person who had the care collected said, "Why, I do feel better. I think I can handle the problem much better now. It really works!"

Word spread. Soon there was a throng of people who came to give their cares to the care-collector. His spot eventually became the most popular one in the square.

One day a woman came into the village walking very slowly and with considerable difficulty. She seemed so burdened that the villagers took her straight to the care-collector. When he explained to her what kind of collector he was, she began to wail, "Oh, you don't know how many cares and burdens and wounds there are in this world. I have just come from a city where there are more hurt and cares than anywhere else. Everyone suffers and no one has any hope left. The worst part is that the rulers of the city thrive and prosper on the cares of the common people. It is a horrible, desperate place. I just had to leave. It was the only hope I had left," she concluded.

The care-collector looked very solemn. He stood up and lifted his pack in a gesture that was slower and more painful than anyone had ever seen before. After a long silence, he spoke slowly. "I must go there."

The villagers and the woman put up a great protest. They didn't want to lose their care-collector. They were afraid that this city might be too much for him. They begged him to stay.

The old man slipped away in the middle of the night, because he didn't want his departure to be a burden and a sorrow for the people he had helped.

It was not long thereafter when a weary and burdened young man came into the village. The people knew without asking that he'd come from the city. They helped him as best they could, and when he was feeling better, they asked him if he knew about the old man who had left for the city several weeks ago.

"Know him!" the youth replied. "Why the whole city has been talking about him. Haven't you heard?"

"Why, no," the people chorused back, "Tell us what happened."

"This old man came quietly into the city and nobody noticed him, at first," the youth recounted. "Then once in a while you could see him talking to people—mostly listening, really. When a person finished talking to him, he bowed his head and did a funny thing with his hands and the person began to feel better."

"For the first time in a long while," the young man continued, "people in the city began to feel better and have a bit of hope for their own lives."

"Yes, we know. He did that here, too," replied the villagers.

"Well, it didn't take long for the authorities to notice him. They told him to leave and to stop meddling in other people's lives. He simply refused," said the youth from the city.

The young man's eyes became very sad and he sobbed softly in his throat. He continued, "They put him in jail, at first, but even there he collected the cares of the other prisoners. Finally, the rulers decided that he was a subversive threat to their system of order and control. So they had him executed."

The villagers gasped. Some began to cry.

"I am so sorry to bring you this sad news about your friend," said the youth. "He was my friend also. He really, genuinely cared about me."

The youth went on. "I feel better for telling you, painful as it is for us all. You know, it is like what he did before he died, his listening and collecting cares." His voiced trailed off as an idea began to lighten his burden.

"It still works!" he exclaimed. "Collecting cares still works! You can do it for me, and I can do it for you. He only showed us how!"

The young man jumped up, filled with new energy and strength. "I'm going back to the city!"

"But what will you do there?" asked several villagers in unison. "You'll get hurt again. There are too many cares and burdens in that city."

"Exactly! Exactly!" he continued. "That's why I'm going. I will become a care-collector!"

70.
The Wise Man

Anonymous

There's a story about a town fool who asked a local teacher how far it is to heaven and how far it is to hell. The teacher replied, "I do not know for sure."

The fool became indignant and angrily said, "Don't know! Why do people pay you for things you don't know?"

"Well, if I was paid for everything I don't know, I would be very rich," said the teacher. "I'm just paid for the little things I do know."

71.
"Nothing Will Grow There!"

Brian Cavanaugh, T.O.R.

Each summer as I bite into a juicy, homegrown tomato, I think of a humorous event concerning a time, as a seminary student, when three of us sought permission to plant a garden. Our house of studies was located in the downtown area of a large metropolitan city. There wasn't much of a backyard. Actually, it was a stone-covered dirt parking lot with no extra space. However, we carefully planned our garden, taking into account the area that received optimal sunshine.

The three of us approached the superior with our plan for a small area to plant some squash, tomatoes and cucumbers. The only real cost involved was to rent a rake, a pick-ax and a hoe. However, getting the superior's permission would still be difficult. None of us who were involved with this garden project will ever forget his response to our request. With a slightly bored, tilting of his head he glanced at us and abjectly replied, "You're wasting your time. Nothing will ever grow there! But, go ahead if you still want to."

We had received permission from on high! So what if it wasn't enthusiastic. We rented tools; raked four inches of stones into neat walls outlining the garden; hoisted the pick-ax and struck what must have been a former refuse area. A gardener's dream—dark, composted, fertile soil just sitting there waiting to be discovered. We looked at each other with broad grins and repeated in unison, "Ah, nothing will grow there."

As you might have surmised by now, things did grow there, in our garden. In fact, twice we re-staked the tomatoes, topping them off, finally, when they were seven feet tall. They seemed more like tomato trees than plants.

Whenever a group of us from those seminarian days get together, the story of our little garden is re-told. "Nothing will ever grow there!"

Isn't it amazing how much can be learned from planting a garden—about life, about people? How often have you said about another person, whether elderly, middle aged, a teenager, or a child, that nothing will ever grow there? Perhaps all that is needed is for someone to help that person rake away some of the stones that are covering up the rich, fertile soil-of-life, just waiting to be discovered.

72.
Acres of Diamonds

Russell Conwell

A classic American essay, "Acres of Diamonds," was told by Rev. Russell Conwell over five thousand times. The proceeds from this essay's presentations provided the funds needed to establish Temple College, now Temple University.

The story is about a wealthy farmer who was probably the richest man in all of Africa. Hafid owned a large farm with fertile soil, as well as herds of camels and goats, and orchards of dates and figs. One day a wandering holy man visited his farm and mentioned that huge fortunes were being made discovering diamonds—fortunes that were even greater than Hafid's.

This news got Hafid's attention. He inquired from the holy man what diamonds were, and how could he acquire this greater fortune. The holy man said he was not sure of all the details, but he had heard that diamonds were usually found in the white sand of rivers that flowed out from valleys formed by V-shaped mountains.

Hafid was eager to increase his fortune, so he sold his farm, his herds and his orchards. He then set out from his home and began the journey to find his fortune in diamonds. Hafid's travels took him all over Africa, up mountains and down into valleys, without finding so much as one diamond. Finally, deep in despair and frustration, Hafid threw himself off a mountain and died a broken and poor man.

But the story does not end with Hafid. For one day, the farmer who had bought Hafid's land was watering the camels in the river which flowed near the house. When the sun glinted off the stream, he saw a shimmering rainbow glitter from a chipped river rock. It was so pretty that the farmer took it into the house and placed it on a shelf where the afternoon sun would strike it and splash rainbows across the room.

Do you remember the wandering holy man? Well, one day, towards late afternoon, he wandered again upon the farm which Hafid had sold. On entering the house, he was startled by a rainbow dancing across the floor. When the holy man saw that the dancing light was coming out of a rock on the shelf, he exclaimed, "Hafid has returned?"

"Why no," replied the baffled farmer. "What do you mean? I don't understand."

"This . . . this rock is what I mean," the holy man said while pointing to the river rock. "Has Hafid returned?"

The farmer laughed as he hefted the rock. "This!" he said, "Why this is just a pretty rock I found out back in the river. I liked the way rainbows seem to dance out from it when the sun strikes it."

Examining the rock more closely, the holy man became even more animated. "That's a diamond," he excitedly told the farmer. "I'm sure of it. Where did you say you found it?"

Somewhat confused with the flurry of excitement, the farmer explained that he found the rock out in the river.

"Show me," insisted the holy man.

The two of them went out back to the river, which flowed out from a valley formed by a V-shaped mountain. And there, in the white sands, they found a larger diamond, then another, and more diamonds, large and small. Actually, the land, which Hafid sold to pursue his fortune elsewhere, turned out to be acres and acres of diamonds. In fact, it became one of the richest diamond mines in all of Africa.

73.
Know When to Change Course

Frank Koch

Two battleships assigned to the training squadron had been at sea on maneuvers in heavy weather for several days.

71

The visibility was poor with patchy fog, so the captain remained on the bridge keeping an eye on all activities.

Shortly after dark, the lookout on the wing of the bridge reported, "Light, bearing on the starboard bow."

"Is it steady or moving astern?" the captain called out.

The lookout replied, "Steady, captain," which meant it was on a dangerous collision course with their ship.

The captain then shouted to the signalman, "Signal the ship: We are on a collision course. Advise you to change course 20 degrees."

Back came a signal, "Advisable for you to change course 20 degrees!"

In reply, the captain said, "Send: I'm a ship's captain. Change course 20 degrees, now!"

"I'm a seaman second class," came the reply. "You had better change course 20 degrees, now!"

By that time, the captain was furious. He spit out a command, "Send: This is a battleship. Change your course immediately."

Back came the flashing light's reply, "This is a lighthouse!"

The battleship changed course.

74.
Words Disclose the Mystery

Thomas Merton

The purpose of a fish trap is to catch fish. When the fish are caught, the trap is forgotten. The purpose of a rabbit snare is to catch rabbits. When the rabbits are caught, the snares are forgotten. The purpose of a word is to convey ideas. When the ideas are grasped, the words are forgotten. Where can I find a person who has forgotten the words? That is the person with whom I would like to talk.

The purpose of a prayer is to enter the presence of God.

When one enters God's presence, the words of prayer are forgotten.

75.
Keeper of the Springs

Anonymous

There was a quiet forest dweller who lived high above an Austrian village along the eastern slope of the Alps. The old gentleman had been hired many years ago by an earlier town council to clear away the debris of leaves and branches from the pristine springs up in the mountain ravines. These springs fed the pool from which the town gathered its water supply via a canal system.

With faithful regularity, the old man patrolled the nearby hills, removed leaves and branches, and cleared away the silt that otherwise would have clogged and contaminated the fresh flow of water. In time, the village became a popular tourist attraction and a favorite spot for vacationers. Graceful swans floated along the canals. The mill wheels from many businesses cranked day and night, farmlands were irrigated, and the view from the village was postcard picturesque.

Years passed. One evening at a town council meeting assembled to review the budget, one member noticed the salary figure contracted to the obscure keeper of the springs. The treasurer questioned the expense and asked, "Who is this old man? Why do we keep him on salary year after year? Has anyone ever seen him?" The treasurer went on, "For all we know, the strange ranger of the hills might be dead. Anyway, he isn't needed any longer." So by unanimous vote, the council dispensed with the old guardian's services.

For several weeks nothing changed. However, by early autumn, the trees began to shed their leaves. Small branches snapped off and fell into the springs hindering the rushing flow of sparkling water. Then, one afternoon someone noticed a slight yellowish-brown tint in the pool. A few days later, the water was much darker. Within another week, a slimy slick covered sections of the water along the canal banks, and a foul odor was soon detected. The mill wheels slowly ground to a halt. The swans left, as did the tourists. Clammy fingers of disease and sickness crept deeply into the heart of the village.

Quickly, an embarrassed town council called a special meeting. Realizing their gross error in judgment to save some money, they rehired the old keeper of the springs, and within several weeks, the sparkling river of life began to clear up. The mill wheels cranked again, and renewed life returned to the village in the Alps.

And what was the name of the Keeper of the Springs? According to town records his name is (Integrity, Joshua, Jesus, Prayer). Are you in need of such a guardian?

76.
Few Recognized Themselves

Anonymous

The famous American cartoonist Thomas Nast was at a party with some friends. Somebody suggested that he draw caricatures of everyone at the party.

Using swift, bold strokes of his pencil, Nast made quick sketches of each person. He passed the sketches around for everyone to look at. There were lots of laughing and joking. Then something unexpected happened. It seems that everyone recognized everyone else, but few recognized themselves.

When it comes to self-recognition, we seem to have a blind spot. We don't see ourselves as clearly as others see us. We just don't recognize our main characteristics—our strengths and our weaknesses—as they really are.

77.
Ugly Duckling?

Anonymous

A young girl was depressed because she was not beautiful. She was discouraged, but as she grew older, her attitude changed. "I realized that not being beautiful was actually a blessing in disguise," she said. "It forced me to develop inner resources and strength. I came to understand that women who can't lean on their beauty must work harder to have the advantage."

Golda Meir went on to become the first woman prime minister of Israel. She not only accepted herself, but rejoiced in who she was.

78.
Work with Flaws

Anonymous

There is a story about two men, both Italian sculptors and contemporaries, named Donatello and Michelangelo. One day Donatello received delivery of a huge block of marble. After examining it carefully, Donatello rejected the marble because it was too flawed and cracked for him to use.

Now this was long before forklifts and hydraulic lifts, so the workmen moved the heavy load by using a series of log rollers. Rather than struggle back to the quarry, the quick-thinking haulers decided to deliver it down the street to Michelangelo. After all, he was known to be a little absent-minded. He might not realize that he had not ordered a three-ton block of marble.

When Michelangelo inspected the marble, he saw the same cracks and flaws, as did Donatello. But he also saw the block as a challenge to his artistic skills. It became a personal challenge he could not pass up. So Michelangelo accepted the block of marble that Donatello had already rejected as too flawed and too cracked to be of any use.

Michelangelo proceeded to carve from that seemingly useless block of marble what is considered to be one of the world's greatest art treasures—the statue "David."

79.
Believe It, Achieve It

Mark Link, S.J.

In the "Star War" movie, *The Empire Strikes Back,* Luke Skywalker flies his X-wing ship to a swamp planet on a personal quest. There he seeks out a Jedi master named Yoda to teach him the ways of becoming a Jedi warrior. Luke wants to free the galaxy from the oppression of the evil tyrant, Darth Vader.

Yoda reluctantly agrees to help Luke and begins by teaching him how to lift rocks with his mental powers.

Then, one day, Yoda tells Luke to lift his ship out from the swamp where it sank after a crash landing. Luke complains that lifting rocks is one thing, but lifting a star-fighter is quite another matter. Yoda insists. Luke manages a valiant effort but fails in his attempt.

Yoda then focuses his mind, and lifts out the ship with ease. Luke, dismayed, exclaims, "I don't believe it!"

"That's why you couldn't lift it," Yoda replied. "You didn't believe you could."

80.
A Life Worth Living?

Anonymous

A man risked his life by swimming through the treacherous rip-tide to save a youngster being swept out to sea.

After the child recovered from the harrowing experience, he said to the man, "Thank you for saving my life."

The man looked into the boy's eyes and said, "That's okay, kid. Just make sure your life was worth saving."

81.
Three Stages in Life
Anonymous

In each person's life there are three stages. When one was young, people said, "He will do something." As he grew older and did nothing, they said, "He could do something if he found himself." When he was white-haired, people said of him, "He might have done something if he had tried anything."

82.
Prince with a Crooked Back
Anonymous

There once was a handsome prince who had a crooked back. This defect kept him from attaining his full potential as the kind of prince he dreamt to be. One day the king had the best sculptor in the land carve a statue of the prince. It portrayed him, however, not with a crooked back but with a straight back. The king placed the statue in the prince's private garden. And whenever the prince gazed at it, his heart would quicken.

Months passed, and people began to say, "Do you notice, the prince's back doesn't seem as crooked as it was."

When the prince overheard this remark, he gained more confidence in himself. Now he began to spend hours studying the statue and meditating on his personal dream. Then one day a remarkable thing happened. The prince reached high overhead, stretching himself. Suddenly, he was standing straight and tall, just like the statue.

You, too, were born to royalty, to be a prince or a princess. But is there a defect keeping you from attaining your full potential as the kind of person you dream to be?

83.
Jump Just So High
Zig Ziglar

Zig Ziglar relates that flea trainers have observed a predictable and strange habit of fleas while training them. When fleas are first put into a jar you can bend over and observe them jumping out of the jar. Of course, fleas are known to be incredible jumpers.

The training begins when the lid is put on the jar. The fleas continue to jump, but now they hit their heads on the lid, over and over again. As you continue to watch them jump and hit the lid, something very interesting happens. The fleas continue their jumping, but they no longer jump high enough to hit the jar lid.

The flea trainer can then remove the lid from the jar. The fleas will continue jumping, but they will not jump out of the jar. Actually, they won't jump out because they no longer can jump out. Why? The reason is simple. They have conditioned themselves to jump only so high. And, once they have conditioned themselves to jump just so high, that's all they can do!

Are you like a flea? Have you been conditioned to jump only so high?

84.
Satan's Strategy
St. Ignatius

St. Ignatius proposed this question to his students, "What strategy would Satan use to seduce people and get them to follow him?"

He concludes: "First, Satan would lead people from a legitimate striving for security to a wrongful striving after money—greed. Second, Satan would lead people from a legitimate striving for acceptance to a wrongful striving after recognition—honor. Finally, Satan would lead people from a legitimate appreciation of their self-worth to sinful self-indulgence—pride. Thus, Satan's strategy is to seduce people gradually, leading them from legitimate self-striving to sinful self-indulgence."

85.
Who Really Loves God?
Anonymous

An angel was walking down the street of a nearby town. In the angel's right hand was a torch and in the left was a bucket of water. "What are you going to do with that fire and water?" a passerby inquired.

The angel replied, "With the torch, I'm going to burn down the mansions of heaven, and with the bucket of water, I'm going to put out the fires of hell. Then we'll see who really loves God."

86.
Never Too Young, Never Too Old
Anonymous

The quality of life is not a chronological matter. Before deciding if you are too young or too old to try a new adventure, or to face new challenges, it might be wise to consider the lives of a few people who didn't let age interfere with their achievement.

— George Burns won his only Oscar at eighty.
— Golda Meir was seventy-one when she became prime minister of Israel.

— Mozart was seven when his first composition was published.
— Grandma Moses didn't start painting until she was eighty. She completed over 1,500 paintings during the remainder of her life, with 25 percent of them produced after she was one hundred years old.
— Benjamin Franklin published his first newspaper column when he was sixteen, and helped frame the U.S. Constitution when he was eighty-one.
— Michelangelo was seventy-one when he painted the Sistine Chapel.
— S.I. Hayakawa retired as president of San Francisco State University at seventy, and was then elected to the U.S. Senate.
— Casey Stengel didn't retire from the rigorous demands of managing the N.Y. Mets until he was seventy-five years old.

87.
Influencing Others
Anonymous

Bubba Smith, former college and pro-football star, is also famous for his beer commercials.

In October 1985, Michigan State honored Bubba by making him the grand marshal of its homecoming parade. Bubba was thrilled to be back at his alma mater. As he rode through the student-lined streets, one side started shouting, "Tastes great!" Students on the other side shouted back, "Less filling!" It was obvious that Bubba's beer commercials were a hit.

Also very obvious that night was the fact that Bubba was deeply disturbed by the number of students at the parade who were "drunk out of their minds." Then and there he made a decision to stop making the beer commercials. He feared that they were influencing young people to do something of which he did not want to be a part. The decision personally cost Bubba a lot of money, but he thought something more important was at stake.

88.
The Disciples Finished the Work
Anonymous

Composer Giacomo Puccini wrote a number of famous operas. In 1922 he was suddenly stricken by cancer while working on his last opera, *Turandot*, which many now consider his best. Puccini said to his students, "If I don't finish *Turandot*, I want you to finish it for me." Shortly afterward he died.

Puccini's students studied the opera carefully and soon completed it. In 1926 the world premiere of *Turandot* was performed in Milan with Puccini's favorite student, Arturo Toscanini, directing. Everything went beautifully until the opera reached the point where Puccini had been forced to put down his pen. Tears ran down Toscanini's face. He stopped the music, put down his baton, turned to the audience, and cried out, "Thus far the Master wrote, but he died."

A vast silence filled the opera house. Then Toscanini picked up the baton again, smiled through his tears, and exclaimed, "But the disciples finished his work."

When *Turandot* ended, the audience broke into thunderous applause. No one at the premiere ever forgot that moment.

89.
Describe What You Saw
Anonymous

The scoutmaster used to take his troop on hikes along wilderness nature trails. After each hike he would challenge the scouts to describe what they had observed on their excursion.

The boys invariably hadn't seen a fraction of what the scoutmaster had seen. He would wave his arms in great circles and shout, "Creation is all around you, but you are blocking it out. Stop wearing your raincoat in the shower. You were born to look, but you have to learn to see!"

90.
Shrine of Learning and Wisdom

Brian Cavanaugh, T.O.R.

There once was a new student starting her freshman year at the "College Among the Pines." She seemed lost, or maybe, searching for something.

A passing senior asked if she could be of any help. "Tell me," asked the freshman, "where can I find the shrine of learning and wisdom? I've looked on my campus map, but I can't locate it."

"Open your eyes, breathe deeply, listen carefully, and focus your attention," the senior told the freshman. She continued, "There is no shrine for learning and wisdom. It is all around you, among the people, the classrooms, the pines. You are already at the place of learning and wisdom!"

91.
Dig a Little Deeper

Anonymous

There's a story about the California gold rush that tells of two brothers who sold all they had and went prospecting for gold. They discovered a vein of the shining ore, staked a claim, and proceeded to get down to the serious business of getting the gold ore out of the mine. All went well at first, but then a strange thing happened. The vein of gold ore disappeared! They had come to the end of the rainbow, and the pot of gold was no longer there. The brothers continued to pick away, but without success. Finally, they gave up in disgust.

They sold their equipment and claim rights for a few hundred dollars, and took the train back home. Now the man who bought the claim hired an engineer to examine the rock strata of the mine. The engineer advised him to continue digging in the same spot where the former owners had left off. And three feet deeper, the new owner struck gold.

A little more persistence and the two brothers would have been millionaires themselves. Thar's gold in you too. Do you need to dig three feet farther?

92.
Yelling Tends to Kill

Anonymous

A story is told about the Solomon Islands where some villagers practice a unique form of logging. If a tree is too large to be felled with an axe, the natives cut it down by yelling at it. You see, woodsmen with special powers creep up on a tree at dawn, surround it, and scream at the top of their lungs. They continue this for 30 days. The tree dies and falls over. The theory is that hollering kills the spirit of the tree. According to the villagers, it always works.

Ah, those poor, innocent natives. Such quaint jungle-lore. Screaming at trees, indeed. How primitive. Too bad they don't have the advantages of modern society and advanced technology.

Me, yell? Well, I've yelled at my family. I've yelled at the telephone and the television. And I've sure yelled a lot while using the computer.

The lady next door yells a lot. Last week I heard her yell while washing windows. Have you noticed that we modern, urbane sophisticates yell at traffic lights and umpires, bills and bank machines? It seems that machines and relatives bear the brunt of most of our yelling.

I don't know what good all that yelling does. Machines and things just sit there. Even kicking doesn't always help. As for people, well, the Solomon Islanders may have a point. Yelling at living things does tend to kill their spirit. Sticks and stones may break our bones, but words will break our hearts.

93.
Doing Good Without Knowing It
Anonymous

An old Sufi story tells of a good man who was granted one wish by God. The man said he would like to go about doing good without knowing about it. God granted his wish.

God decided it was such a good idea, that He granted the same wish to all human beings. So it was, and so it is to this day.

94.
Success or Failure
Anonymous

A troubled man made an appointment with a rabbi. He was a wise and gentle rabbi. "Rabbi," said the man, wringing his hands, "I'm a failure. More than half the time I do not succeed in doing what I know I must."

"Oh," murmured the rabbi.

"Please say something wise, rabbi," pleaded the man.

After much pondering, the rabbi replied, "Ah, my son, I give you this bit of wisdom: Go and look on page 930 of *The New York Times Almanac* for the year 1970, and maybe you will find peace of mind."

Confused by such strange advice, the troubled man went to the library to look up the source. And this is what he found—lifetime batting averages for the world's greatest baseball players. Ty Cobb, the greatest slugger of them all, had a lifetime average of .367. Even the King of Swat, Babe Ruth, didn't do that well.

So the man returned to the rabbi and questioned, "Ty Cobb, .367. That's it?"

"Correct," countered the rabbi. "Ty Cobb, .367. He got a hit once out of every three times at bat. He didn't even hit .500. *So what do you expect already?*"

"Aha," said the man, who thought he was a wretched failure because he succeeded only half the time at what he must do.

Theology is amazing. Holy books abound, even where we don't expect them.

95.
Hearing Problem?

Anonymous

There was a woman who believed she had a hearing problem. Her friends kept telling her she had a problem. She was always asking them to repeat what had been said in a conversation.

The woman made an appointment with an audiologist to check out her hearing problem. The doctor told her that he had the latest diagnostic technology, but that he preferred using his old reliable test first. So the doctor took out his railroad pocket watch.

Seated across from the woman, the doctor held up the watch and asked her if she could hear the watch's ticking. "Sure, just fine," she replied. So the doctor got up, walked behind her and asked if she could hear it now. Again she gave an affirmative response. The doctor then walked across the office, standing about 20 feet away and asked if the ticking could still be heard. The woman replied that she heard it easily. Finally, the doctor walked out the door so he was out of sight, and asked if she could still hear the watch. Again the woman said that she heard it clearly.

The doctor returned to his chair putting the old, reliable watch back in his pocket. Looking at the woman he gave her his diagnosis. "Your hearing is perfect," the doctor said. "Your problem is not in your hearing; you just don't know how to listen."

96.
Acorns and Pumpkins
Anonymous

An old poem describes a woman walking through a meadow, meditating on nature. While strolling about, she came upon a field of golden pumpkins. In the corner of the field stood a majestic, huge oak tree.

She sat under the oak tree musing on the strange twists in nature which put tiny acorns on huge branches and huge pumpkins on tiny vines. She thought to herself, "God blundered with Creation! He should have put the small acorns on the tiny vines and the large pumpkins on the huge branches."

Nodding off, the woman stretched out under the oak tree for a nap. A few minutes after falling asleep she was awakened by a tiny acorn bouncing off her nose. Chuckling to herself, she rubbed her nose and thought, "Maybe God was right after all!"

97.
New, Pew, or Seed Potato
Rev. George White

A Pew Potato wants to be cared for, but doesn't know how to care. A Pew Potato wants to be visited, but never visits. A Pew Potato wants the benefits of Bible study, but leaves the studying to others.

A Pew Potato catalogues the faults of others, but overlooks his or her own. A Pew Potato has not only forgotten who he or she used to be, but has also lost sight of who he or she could yet become.

New Potatoes become Pew Potatoes when they stop growing and just vegetate. But Pew Potatoes can become Seed Potatoes when they get out of their skins, die to themselves, and sprout anew.

98.
Cost of Apathy

Anonymous

If you place a frog into a pot of cold water, the frog will happily swim around. That's not very surprising. Frogs like cold water.

But, if you place a frog into a pot of boiling water, the frog will try to jump out. That's not too surprising either. Frogs don't like boiling water.

However, here's what is surprising. If you place a frog into a pot of cold water, then gradually turn up the heat until the water boils, the frog will make no attempt to jump out of the pot. It slowly adapts itself to the change—adapts itself to death.

99.
El Dorado—Treasure Within

Herbert D. Seibert

El Dorado, a country wealthy beyond all desires in gold and treasure, lies at every person's door. Your bonanza lies under your very own feet. Your luck is ready at hand. All is within, nothing is without. Each person individually and collectively is entitled to life in all its abundance. It is a most evident truth of wisdom. Religion and philosophy assert it; history and science prove it. "That they might have life, and have it more abundantly," is the law.

What do you seek in life? Pay the price, and take it as yours. There is no limit to the supply, but the more precious the thing you seek, the greater the price.

Where to find the gold of El Dorado? The gold of the spirit is secured when each person finds himself or herself. Along with the discovery of self, he or she finds freedom, achievement, prosperity and life's riches.

Let each person seek the El Dorado within. Inner power is plentiful; the source is inexhaustible. As the early religious teachers expressed it, that which is received is according to the measure of the recipient. It is not the power that is lacking; it is the will. When an individual finds oneself, the will automatically becomes set toward El Dorado.

100.
The Pig and the Cow
Anonymous

"Why is it," said the rich man to his minister, "that people call me stingy when everyone knows that when I die I'm leaving everything to the church?"

"Let me tell you a fable about the pig and the cow," said the minister. "The pig was unpopular while the cow was beloved. This puzzled the pig. 'People speak warmly of your gentle nature and your sorrowful eyes,' the pig said to the cow. 'They think you're generous because each day you give them milk and cream. But what about me? I give them everything I have. I give bacon and ham. I provide bristles for brushes. They even pickle my feet! Yet no one likes me. Why is that?' "

"Do you know what the cow answered?" said the minister. "The cow said, 'Perhaps it is because I give while I'm still living.' "

Source Acknowledgments

This book is the fruition of years of reading, listening and transcribing stories from many and varied sources. I thank the authors and publishers who have given their generous cooperation and permission to include these stories in this collection. Further reproduction without permission is prohibited.

Every effort has been made to acknowledge the proper source for each story; regrettably, I am unable to give proper credit to every story. When the proper source becomes known, proper credit will be given in future editions of this book.

Understanding that there is a need for a reading list of sources for stories and illustrations I have included a "Further Reading" list of books that I have found helpful. The reading list is prior to the theme index for this book.

THE EAGLE AND THE RATTLESNAKE
Anonymous
Source Unknown

THE PLIMSOLL LINE
Anonymous
Source Unknown

LISTENING ... PAYING ATTENTION!
Hank Ketcham
Source Unknown

ARE YOU JESUS?
    Brennan Manning
    Source Unknown

DO SOMETHING SO MUCH
    Anonymous
    Source Unknown

TO HAVE A BRILLIANT SON
    Chaim Potok
    Source Unknown

BLACK PEBBLE ... WHITE PEBBLE?
    Anonymous
    Source Unknown

IN THE PROCESS OF TRYING
    Anonymous
    Source Unknown

FOCUS YOUR THINKING
    Anonymous
    Source Unknown

ANANIAS THE COBBLER (ADAPTED)
    David Juniper
    Along the Water's Edge
    NY: Paulist Press, 1982

TWO MONKS TRAVELING
    Anonymous
    Source Unknown

JESUS' AND JUDAS' FACES
    Anonymous
    Source Unknown

SHOES ON A GOOSE
Anonymous
Source Unknown

LET THE MUSIC OUT
Anonymous
Source Unknown

WALKING WITH THE LORD
David Juniper
Along the Water's Edge
Paulist Press, 1982

COURAGE OR COMFORT
Anonymous
Source Unknown

BLESSING IN DISGUISE
Anonymous
Source Unknown

LIBERAL ARTS EDUCATION
James Michener
Source Unknown

A PRAYER FOR HIS SON
Gen. Douglas MacArthur
Source Unknown

GOD, HEAR ME
G. Ray Funkhouser
Insight, #60
Excerpted with permission from *Insight®*,
the monthly audiocassette program by Nightingale-
Conant Corp., 7300 North Lehigh Ave., Chicago, IL
60648, 1–800–572–2770

THE GIFT OF THE MAGI (ADAPTED)
O. Henry
Source Unknown

THE FOURTH WISE MAN
Henry Van Dyke
Source Unknown

A LEADER'S IMPACT
Anonymous
Source Unknown

NEED TO ASK OTHERS
Anonymous
Source Unknown

THE LION AND THE BULL
Anonymous
Source Unknown

KNOW THE SHEPHERD
Anonymous
The Priest, December 1987, page 14

BRAVERY? . . . NEW BRAKES!
Mike Wickett
Insight, #62
Excerpted with permission from *Insight*®,
the monthly audiocassette program by Nightingale-
Conant Corp., 7300 North Lehigh Ave., Chicago, IL
60648, 1–800–572–2770

DON'T REST ON LAURELS
Anonymous
Source Unknown

THE GREAT STONE FACE
    Nathaniel Hawthorne
    Source Unknown

TRANSFORMATION TO NEW LIFE (ADAPTED)
    Cecil B. De Mille
    Source Unknown

BECOME WHAT YOU WANT TO BE
    Anonymous
    Source Unknown

LIFE IS A STRUGGLE
    Anonymous
    Source Unknown

MAP MAKERS AND DRAGONS
    Roger Von Oech
    Source Unknown

EXCUSES
    Theophane the Monk
    Tales of a Magic Monastery
    NY: Crossroad, 1987

REFINING GOLD
    Anonymous
    Source Unknown

THE MISSIONARY'S SUNDIAL
    Anonymous
    Source Unknown

DESIRE DOES MAKE A DIFFERENCE
    Zig Ziglar
    Source Unknown

HOW TO CATCH MONKEYS
  Anonymous
  Source Unknown

SITTING THIS ONE OUT
  Anonymous
  Source Unknown

SPARKY—CHARLIE BROWN
  Earl Nightingale
  Earl Nightingale's Greatest Discovery
  NY: Dodd, Mead & Co., 1987

THE MONK'S VISION
  Lawrence Le Shan
  Source Unknown

SECRET OF HAPPINESS
  Anonymous
  Source Unknown

THE LITTLE GUY WITH A BIG DREAM
  Donna Menis
  Personal Correspondence

POWER OF COMPASSION
  Fr. Jim McNamara
  Will the Real Me Please Stand Up?
  Allen, TX: Argus Communications, 1985

THE FROG PRINCE
  David K. Reynolds, Ph.D.
  Playing Ball On Running Water
  NY: Quill Books, 1984

ACRES OF DIAMONDS
Russell Conwell
"Acres of Diamonds" essay

KNOW WHEN TO CHANGE COURSE
Frank Koch
Forbes, Feb. 20, 1989

WORDS DISCLOSE THE MYSTERY
Thomas Merton
The Way of Chuang Tzu
NY: New Directions, 1965

KEEPER OF THE SPRINGS
Anonymous
Source Unknown

FEW RECOGNIZED THEMSELVES
Anonymous
Source Unknown

UGLY DUCKLING?
Anonymous
Source Unknown

WORK WITH FLAWS
Anonymous
Source Unknown

BELIEVE IT, ACHIEVE IT
Mark Link, S.J.
Challenge
Allen, TX: Tabor Publishing, 1988

A LIFE WORTH LIVING?
    Anonymous
    Source Unknown

THREE STAGES IN LIFE
    Anonymous
    Source Unknown

PRINCE WITH A CROOKED BACK
    Anonymous
    Source Unknown

JUMP JUST SO HIGH
    Zig Ziglar
    See You at the Top
    Gretna, LA: Pelican Publishing, 1977

SATAN'S STRATEGY
    St. Ignatius
    Source Unknown

WHO REALLY LOVES GOD?
    Anonymous
    Source Unknown

NEVER TOO YOUNG, NEVER TOO OLD
    Anonymous
    Source Unknown

INFLUENCING OTHERS
    Anonymous
    Source Unknown

THE DISCIPLES FINISHED THE WORK
    Anonymous
    Source Unknown

COST OF APATHY
Anonymous
Source Unknown

EL DORADO—TREASURE WITHIN
Herbert D. Seibert
Source Unknown

THE PIG AND THE COW
Anonymous
Source Unknown

Further Reading

Aesop's Fables. London: Bracken Books, 1986.

Applebaum, Rabbi Morton and Silver, Rabbi Samuel M. eds. *Speak to the Children of Israel.* KTAV Publishing House, Inc., 1976.

Aurelio, John. *Story Sunday.* New York: Paulist Press, 1978.

———. *Fables for God's People.* New York: Crossroad, 1988.

Ausubel, Nathan, ed. *A Treasury of Jewish Folklore.* NY: Crown Publishers, 1948.

Barker Esther T. *The Unused Cradle.* Nashville: The Upper Room, 1968.

Bausch, William. *Storytelling: Imagination and Faith.* Mystic, CT: Twenty-Third Publications, 1984.

Bell, Martin. *The Way of the Wolf: Stories, Poems, Songs and Thoughts on the Parables of Jesus.* New York: Ballantine Books/Epiphany Edition, 1983.

Benjamin, Don-Paul and Ron Miner. *Come Sit With Me Again: Sermons for Children.* New York: The Pilgrim Press, 1987.

Bettelheim, Bruno. *The Uses of Enchantment.* New York: Vintage Books, 1977.

Bodo, O.F.M., Murray. *Tales of St. Francis: Ancient Stories for Contemporary Living.* New York: Doubleday, 1988.

Boyer, Mark. *Following the Star: Daily Reflections for Advent and Christmas.* Liguori, MO: Liguori Publications, 1989.

Brunvand, Jan Harold. *Curses! Broiled Again!* NY: W.W. Norton & Co., 1989.

Buber, Martin. *Tales of the Hasidim: Early Masters.* NY: Schocken Books, 1975.

———. *Tales of the Hasidim: Later Masters.* NY: Schocken Books, 1948.

Bushnaq, Inea, ed. *Arab Folktales*. NY: Random House (Pantheon Books), 1986.

Byrd, Charles W. *The Fall of the Sparrow*. Lima, OH: C.S.S. Publishing Company, Inc., 1990.

Carroll, James. *Wonder and Worship*. New York: Newman Press, 1970.

Cassady, Marsh. *Storytelling: Step by Step*. San Jose, CA: Resource Publications, 1990.

Castagnola, S.J., Larry. *More Parables for Little People*. San Jose, CA: Resource Publications, Inc, 1987.

Cattan, Henry. *The Garden of Joys: An Anthology of Oriental Anecdotes, Fables and Proverbs*. London: Namara Publications, Ltd, 1979.

Cavanaugh, Brian, T.O.R. *The Sower's Seeds: One Hundred Inspiring Stories for Preaching, Teaching and Public Speaking*. Mahwah, NJ: Paulist Press, 1990.

Chappell, Stephen, O.S.B. *Dragons & Demons, Angels & Eagles: Morality Tales for Teens*. St. Louis: Liguori Publications, 1990.

Colainni, James F., ed. *Sunday Sermons Treasury of Illustrations*. Pleasantville, NJ: Voicings Publications, 1982.

Complete Grimm's Fairy Tales, The. New York: Pantheon Books, 1972.

Cornils, Stanley, ed. *34 Two-Minute Talks for Youth and Adults*. Cincinnati, OH: Standard Publications, 1985.

de Mello, Anthony, S.J. *The Song of the Bird*. India: Gujarat Sahitya Prakash, 1982.

———. *One Minute Wisdom*. New York: Doubleday & Co, 1986.

———. *Taking Flight*. New York: Doubleday, 1988.

———. *The Heart of the Enlightened*. New York: Doubleday, 1989.

Doleski, Teddi. *The Hurt*. Mahwah, NJ: Paulist Press, 1983.

———. *Silvester and the Oogaloo Boogaloo*. Mahwah, NJ: Paulist Press, 1990.

Fahy, Mary. *The Tree That Survived the Winter*. Mahwah, NJ: Paulist Press, 1989.

Field, Claud, trans. *Jewish Legends of the Middle Ages.* London: Shapiro Vallentine & Co.

Giono, Jean. *The Man Who Planted Trees.* Vermont: Chelsea Green Publishing Co., 1985.

Hasler, Richard A. *God's Game Plan: Sports Anecdotes for Preachers.* Lima, OH: C.S.S. Publishing Company, Inc., 1990.

Haugaard, Erik Christian, trans. *Hans Christian Andersen: The Complete Fairy Tales and Stories.* NY: Doubleday (Anchor Books), 1974.

Haviland, Virginia, ed. *North American Legends.* New York: Philomel Books, 1979.

Hays, Edward. *Twelve And One-Half Keys.* Easton, KS: Forest of Peace Books, 1981.

―――. *The Ethiopian Tattoo Shop.* Easton, KS: Forest of Peace Books, 1983.

―――. *A Pilgrim's Almanac: Reflections for Each Day of the Year.* Easton, KS: Forest of Peace Books, 1989.

Holdcraft, Paul E., ed. *Snappy Stories for Sermons and Speeches.* Nashville: Abingdon Press, 1987.

Johnson, Barry L. *The Visit of the Tomten.* Nashville: The Upper Room, 1981.

Johnson, Miriam. *Inside Twenty-Five Classic Children's Stories.* New York: Paulist Press, 1986.

Juknialis, Joseph. *Winter Dreams and other such friendly dragons.* San Jose, CA: Resource Publications, Inc, 1979.

Killinger, John. *Parables for Christmas.* Nashville: Abingdon Press, 1985.

Kronberg, Ruthilde and McKissack, Patricia C. *A Piece of the Wind and Other Stories to Tell.* NY: Harper & Row, 1990.

Levin, Meyer. *Classic Hasidic Tales.* New York: Dorset Press, 1985.

Lieberman, Leo and Beringause, Arthur. *Classics of Jewish Literature.* Secaucus, NJ: Book Sales, Inc., 1988.

Loder, Ted. *Tracks in the Snow: Tales Spun from the Manger*. San Diego, CA: LuraMedia, 1985.

Lufburrow, Bill. *Illustrations Without Sermons*. Nashville: Abingdon Press, 1985.

Marbach, Ethel. *The White Rabbit: A Franciscan Christmas Story*. Cincinnati, OH: St. Anthony Messenger Press, 1984.

McArdle, Jack. *150 Stories for Preachers and Teachers*. Mystic, CT: Twenty-Third Publications, 1990.

Miller, Donald. *The Gospel and Mother Goose*. Elgin, IL: Brethren Press, 1987.

Newcombe, Jack. *A Christmas Treasury*. New York: Viking Press, 1982.

Nomura, Yushi. *Desert Wisdom: Sayings from the Desert Fathers*. New York: Image Books, 1984.

O'Connor, Ulick. *Irish Tales & Sagas*. London: Dragon Books, 1985.

O'Faolain, Eileen. *Irish Sagas and Folk Tales*. New York: Avenel Books, 1982.

Olszewski, Daryl. *Balloons! Candy! Toys! and Other Parables for Storytellers*. San Jose, CA: Resource Publications, 1986.

Opie, Iona & Peter. *The Classic Fairy Tales*. New York: Oxford University Press, 1974.

Paulus, Trina. *Hope for the Flowers*. NJ: Paulist Press, 1972.

Pennel, Jr., Joe E. *The Whisper of Christmas: Reflections for Advent and Christmas*. Nashville: The Upper Room, 1984.

Powers, C.P., Isaias. *Nameless Faces in the Life of Jesus*. Mystic, CT: Twenty-Third Publications, 1981.

———. *Father Ike's Stories for Children*. Mystic, CT: Twenty-Third Publications, 1988.

Reynolds, David K., Ph.D. *Playing Ball on Running Water*. New York: Quill, 1984.

———. *Even in Summer the Ice Doesn't Melt*. NY: Quill, 1986.

————. *Water Bears No Scars*. New York: Quill, 1987.

————. *Pools of Lodging for the Moon: Strategy for a Positive Life-Style*. NY: William Morrow & Co., 1989.

————. *A Thousand Waves: A Sensible Life-Style for Sensitive People*. NY: William Morrow & Co., 1990.

Seuss, Dr. *Oh, the Places You'll Go!* New York: Random House, 1990.

Singer, Isaac Bashevis. *Stories for Children*. New York: Farrar, Straus, Giroux, 1984.

————. *The Image and Other Stories*. London: Jonathan Cape, Ltd., 1985.

Smith, Richard Gordon. *Ancient Tales and Folklore of Japan*. London: Bracken Books, 1986.

Stoddard, Sandol. *The Rules and Mysteries of Brother Solomon*. Mahwah, NJ: Paulist Press, 1987.

Sutherland, Zena and Liningston, Myra Cohn, eds. *The Scott, Foresman Anthology of Children's Literature*. IL: Scott, Foresman and Co., 1984.

Thompson, Stith. *The Folktale*. Los Angeles: The University of California Press, 1977.

Weinreich, Beatrice Silverman, ed. *Yiddish Folktales*. Translated by Leonard Wolf. NY: Pantheon Books (Random House), 1988.

Wharton, Paul, ed. *Stories and Parables for Preachers and Teachers*. New York: Paulist Press, 1986.

White, William R., ed. *Speaking in Stories*. Minneapolis: Augsburg, 1982.

————. *Stories for Telling*. Minneapolis: Augsburg, 1986.

————. *Stories for the Journey*. Minneapolis: Augsburg, 1988.

Wiesel, Elie. *Souls On Fire: Portraits and Legends of Hasidic Masters*. New York: Summit Books, 1972.

————. *Somewhere a Master: Further Hasidic Portraits and Legends*. New York: Summit Books, 1981.

Yolen, Jane, ed. *Favorite Folktales from Around the World*. NY: Pantheon Books, 1986.

Theme Index